W9-ABR-705

PERGAMON INTERNATIONAL LIBRARY
of Science, Technology, Engineering and Social Studies
The 1000-volume original paperback library in aid of education,
industrial training and the enjoyment of leisure
Publisher: Robert Maxwell, M.C.

MENU FRENCH

THE PERGAMON TEXTBOOK
INSPECTION COPY SERVICE

An inspection copy of any book published in the Pergamon International Library will gladly be sent to academic staff without obligation for their consideration for course adoption or recommendation. Copies may be retained for a period of 60 days from receipt and returned if not suitable. When a particular title is adopted or recommended for adoption for class use and the recommendation results in a sale of 12 or more copies, the inspection copy may be retained with our compliments. The Publishers will be pleased to receive suggestions for revised editions and new titles to be published in this important International Library.

International Series in Hospitality Management

Editor-in-Chief: JOHN O'CONNOR, Head, Department of Catering
Management, Oxford Polytechnic, England

Editors: EWOUT CASSEE, Director Higher Hotel School, The Hague,
The Netherlands

GERALD LATTIN, Dean, School of Hospitality Management,
Florida International University, Miami, USA

DONALD SMITH, formerly Principal, College of Catering and
Hospitality Services, Brisbane, Australia

This series aims to reinforce and to extend the body of knowledge of the
profession of hospitality management, a profession which includes the
management of hotels and other forms of accommodation; the
management of catering and of food and beverage service establishments;
and the management of clubs, and conference and holiday centres. The
series will include textbooks, monographs and papers of value in the
education, training and development of students and managers beginning
their careers. It will also provide material for the continuing education of
members of the profession, including managers, teachers and research
workers, through developing their understanding of and effectiveness within
the hospitality industry.

Some Titles in the Series

ATKINSON, D.
Hotel and Catering French

HAYTER, R.
A Career in Catering

The Pergamon Textbook Inspection Copy Service is applicable to both
these books

MENU FRENCH

DAVID ATKINSON

B.A., Ph.D., P.G.C.E.

Senior Lecturer in French,
Oxford Polytechnic, UK

Illustrated by Sharon Ratcliffe

PERGAMON PRESS

OXFORD · NEW YORK · TORONTO · SYDNEY · PARIS · FRANKFURT

U.K.	Pergamon Press Ltd., Headington Hill Hall, Oxford OX3 0BW, England
U.S.A.	Pergamon Press Inc., Maxwell House, Fairview Park, Elmsford, New York 10523, U.S.A.
CANADA	Pergamon of Canada, Suite 104, 150 Consumers Road, Willowdale, Ontario M2J 1P9, Canada
AUSTRALIA	Pergamon Press (Aust.) Pty. Ltd., P.O. Box 544, Potts Point, N.S.W. 2011, Australia
FRANCE	Pergamon Press SARL, 24 rue des Ecoles, 75240 Paris, Cedex 05, France
FEDERAL REPUBLIC OF GERMANY	Pergamon Press GmbH, 6242 Kronberg-Taunus, Hammerweg 6, Federal Republic of Germany

448,002
A z 5 m
11.7436
Mar. 1981

First published in 1978 by Oxford Polytechnic Press

Reprinted with revisions 1979

Reissued 1980 by Pergamon Press, Oxford

British Library Cataloguing in Publication Data

Atkinson, David, *b. 1932*
Menu French. - (International series in hospitality management). - (Pergamon international library).
1. Cookery - Terminology
2. French language
I. Title II. Series
448'.002'4642   TX349   80-40253

ISBN 0-08-024309-6 (hardcover)
ISBN 0-08-024308-8 (Flexicover)

Printed and bound in Great Britain by
William Clowes (Beccles) Limited, Beccles and London

In Memory of my Parents

CONTENTS

FOREWORD

This book is an attempt to clarify a somewhat disorderly situation in the writing of menu French. Mistakes are frequent, not only on the menu card itself but also in reference books, many of which are inconsistent; for example, the same word can appear with a capital letter in one part of the book and a small letter in another part, without apparent reason. Many avoid some of the problems of menu French by using block capitals, but not all the problems can be avoided in this way, and a little time spent studying this book should help such people to face up to the problem before them and overcome it with reasonable confidence. Of course, in all fairness, it should be recognised that such reference books are concerned with the recipe and not with the French. *This book is concerned with the French.*

The two elements of a menu item – the recipe and the French – must, however, go hand in hand, and it is often impossible to correct the French without consulting the recipe. Such research is very time-consuming and it is therefore hoped that this book will be of practical use to those whose lot it is to write out menus. The book is, however, intended primarily as a teaching aid in Hotel and Catering Departments of colleges. Anyone who is required to write menu items, whether on the blackboard or on the menu card, should ensure that the French is correct. Once the principles of correct menu writing are understood, then it is possible to tackle any item and be sure of success. If a dish does not appear in the examples given, then, by consulting the lists in Part Two of the book, the reader will be able to work out the correct form of the item required.

The vocabulary at the end of the book is based on a study of some 6,000 items and is therefore fuller than it would have been if only the examples given in the book had been scrutinised. Where considered appropriate, translations of preparations have been included (translations rather than interpretations). Although 'à la parisienne' may mean more than one thing depending on the dish it is describing (compare, for example, 'Bombe à la parisienne' with 'Poularde à la parisienne'), the reader, seeing that it means 'in Parisian style' will no doubt expect something rather more lavishly prepared than, say, 'à la paysanne' which he sees means 'in peasant style' and which will no doubt lead him to expect a simple dish including a variety of vegetables.

The books most consulted in the preparation of this book are *Hering's Dictionary of*

Classical and Modern Cookery (published by Giessen, 1976; English language version by W. Bickle), *Menu Terminology* by H. C. Clarke (London, 1969), *A Dictionary of Cuisine French* by Steve Combes (London, 1962), *Le Nouveau Larousse Gastronomique* by P. Montagné (édition revue par R. J. Courtine, Paris, 1967), L. Saulnier's *Le Répertoire de la Cuisine* (London, n.d.) and H. Smith's *Classical Recipes of the World and Master Culinary Guide* (London, 1954).

PART ONE

SURVEY OF THE GRAMMATICAL RULES

GOVERNING

THE WRITING OF MENU FRENCH

1. The definite article (le, la, l', les)

The term 'Head Noun' as used in this explanation means the first noun of the item;
the term 'Secondary Noun' means the second noun of the item.

a) Although the definite article before the Head Noun does appear on certain menus,
it is difficult to see any justification for its general use. The definite article serves to
particularise a noun, and its use in, for example, 'Les haricots verts' (*the* French beans)
would for this reason appear erroneous. However, should one *special* item be served
during the course of the meal, and the *whole of this item* be served, then the use of the
definite article could be justified:

> Le dindonneau rôti à l'anglaise

Were the turkey to be carved beforehand and served in portions, the definite article
would not be used. Such mistakes as '*Le* selle d'agneau Maintenon' (taken from a
menu) give a very bad impression, and it would seem advisable to omit the definite
article altogether from the Head Noun.

b) A similar difficulty occurs with the Secondary Noun.

> Raviers *des* hors-d'oeuvre
>
> Purée *des* pommes

are incorrect. Perhaps a simple translation into English is the easiest way of recog-
nising this error. Would one say

> Dishes of *the* hors-d'oeuvre
>
> Purée of *the* apples?

If one did, one would be incorrectly particularising the nouns 'hors-d'oeuvre' and
'apples'. The correct forms, therefore, are

> Raviers de hors-d'oeuvre

and   Purée de pommes

2. The adjective and the number of the noun

a) The adjective agrees with the noun it qualifies. This agreement is generally shown
by the addition of an -e if the noun is feminine singular, of -es if the noun is feminine

plural, and of -s if the noun is masculine plural. There are a number of adjectives which require different modification. Part Two, Section 1, lists the adjectives which are most frequently used in menu French, with their variations and meanings.

b) Care must be taken to identify the noun that is in fact being qualified. In the item
> Selle d'agneau rôtie

it is the word 'selle' and not 'agneau' which the word 'rôtie' qualifies. This will generally be the case with cuts of meat ('filet', 'selle', 'côtelette' etc.).

c) Difficulty arises when deciding whether to put a Head Noun into the singular or the plural. Some nouns obviously go into the singular (e.g., 'oie', 'caneton', 'poulet') whilst others obviously go into the plural (e.g. 'petits pois', 'pommes', 'carottes'). There are several which could do either and circumstances will decide whether the singular or the plural should be used. Whether to write
> Côtelette d'agneau grillée

or   Côtelettes d'agneau grillées

will depend on the number of cutlets being served.

d) Certain nouns require special attention. The word 'suprême' is an example; generally, this word should be put in the plural for it usually refers to the fillets of a fish or the strips of white meat from the breast of poultry. It is, however, also used to denote a dish of great delicacy and must then be used in the singular:
> Suprême de foie gras

Some words such as 'céleris' and 'épinards' which are usually singular in English ('celery' and 'spinach') generally occur in the plural in French, although usage is not consistent:
> Céleris à la grecque
> Salade de céleri

3. Apparent disagreement of the adjective

a) When an adjective formed from the name of a country, region, or town is used, what would at first sight seem a disagreement of the adjective occurs. Examples of this are:

> Canard rouennaise ('canard' is masculine, 'rouennaise' is feminine)
> Petits pois française ('petits pois' is masculine plural, 'française' is feminine
>   singular)

The fact is that these adjectives really refer to a noun that has been omitted, viz., 'la mode'. The expression 'à la mode' does occasionally occur (see p.51) but generally the word 'mode' is omitted and only 'à la' used. The omission of 'à la', which is a common practice, is to be discouraged; the distinction between the place of origin (e.g., 'Boutons bruxellois') and the method of preparation (e.g. 'Filets mignons à la bruxelloise') must be maintained and this cannot be done if 'à la' is omitted indiscriminately. Although not as often used as the feminine singular form (*with* 'à la'), the masculine form has been included in Part Two, section 3, in case it is required.

4. Further remarks concerning the use of 'à la'

a) Not only must one avoid omitting 'à la' when it ought to be used, one must also avoid using 'à la' when it ought *not* to be used. Unfortunately this is a very common error too. Often a dish is dedicated to a particular person, place or event, and to use 'à la' in these circumstances is incorrect. There are, in fact, very few proper nouns which require the use of 'à la'. The following examples may serve to clarify the point:

> Entrecôte Mirabeau (not *à la Mirabeau,* which would mean 'in the style of Mirabeau')
>
> Sole à la Dugléré ('in the style of Dugléré', since Dugléré was the chef)

See p. 19

b) The use of 'à la' (and its other forms 'au', 'à l'', 'aux') meaning 'cooked with', 'flavoured with', or 'accompanied by', as opposed to 'in the style of' should be noted:

> Canapés à l'anguille fumée
>
> Caneton rouennais à la bigarade
>
> Omelette à la ciboulette
>
> Petits pois au fenouil
>
> Poires à la crème
>
> Poularde aux truffes

c) 'A la' and its other forms also serve to describe the method of cooking (or method of serving):

> Bifteck à la poêle
>
> Escalope de ris de veau au gratin
>
> Haddock au four
>
> Langouste à la broche
>
> Lotte au court-bouillon
>
> Pommes à la vapeur
>
> Truffes à la serviette

(See Part Two, Section 4 for a list of further examples of the uses mentioned in these last two sections.)

d) Consider the two items

Purée *de* pommes de terre

and Tarte *aux* pommes

The distinction here is clear; in the first example the purée consists solely of potatoes, whereas in the second example the apples are an addition to the tart which exists in its own right. This could be expressed in English as 'Purée *of* potatoes' and 'Tart *with* apples'. The distinction is not, however, always so clearly drawn:

Potage *de* betterave à la russe

but Potage *au* chou-fleur

and Canapés *aux* anchois

but Canapés *de* langouste

It would seem that, in view of the distinction established, the use of 'de' is incorrect.

5. Capital letters, hyphens, and accents

The presentation of the menu-card is the concern of the hotel or restaurant, not of the French specialist. Nevertheless, it would be fair to criticise the former for excessive use of capitals, omission of hyphens, and use of incorrect accents. In the days of copper-plate writing the capital letter had some aesthetic value and was skilfully drawn to make the menu-card a work of art. If the individual menu item is to be regarded as a title, then the menu writer will feel justified in putting capital letters for all important words in that item; if, however, we take the analogy of the titles of books, French bibliographies tend to list them using a capital letter for the first word only, unless the title is a short one. This would seem to be a good practice. There are rules for the use of capital letters for those who wish to observe them. A menu written in BLOCK CAPITALS is a counsel of despair and has little aesthetic appeal, particularly if the menu-card is small or has a large number of items on it. It is certainly possible for a menu to be correctly written and in accordance with the rules of capitalisation, hyphenation and accentuation and still be of a pleasing appearance.

a) Capital letters

The following basic points can be established:

i. The first letter of a menu item will be a capital letter.

> Darne de cabillaud grillée

ii. No other word will have a capital letter unless it is a proper noun, i.e., the name of *one* place (e.g., Nantua) or of *one* person (e.g., Edouard VII, Brillat-Savarin).

> Glace Plombières   (Place)
>
> Oeufs Parmentier   (Person)

(Part Two, Section 2 gives a list of words requiring capital letters.)

In addition to the two basic points mentioned above, it is useful to note the following points.

i. English people, used to writing the adjective formed from the name of a place with a capital letter (e.g., French, English, Parisian), tend to follow this practice in writing French. This is incorrect and the adjective must always be written with a small letter.

> Grenouilles à l'anglaise   (not 'à l'Anglaise')

ii. When the name of a region, town etc., is used to represent the product of that region or town, then the product is spelled with a small letter (that is, the proper noun becomes a common noun).

> Bordeaux (the region) produces *le* bordeaux (the product)
>
> La Champagne produces *le* champagne (*le* vin)
>
> Camembert produces *le* camembert (*le* fromage)
>
> Roquefort produces *le* roquefort (*le* fromage)

iii. A common feature both in English and in French is for the name of a person to be used to denote an article (examples in English are an albert, a victoria, a negus, a martinet). When this is the case the noun denoting the article is spelled with a small letter. It must not, however, be assumed that *all* proper nouns may be used as common nouns: it is only when such nouns are accepted as common nouns in the language that we may use them in this way.

Examples of proper nouns used as common nouns in menu French are:

une béchamel	une mirepoix
une charlotte	une mornay
une duxelles	un savarin
une julienne	une soubise

Care must be taken to ensure that, in the menu item in question, the common noun is being used. Compare, for example,

Langouste Mornay au gratin (in which 'Mornay' means much more than the addition of a Mornay sauce)

and   Oeufs pochés à la mornay (in which 'mornay' is a common noun and means the addition of a Mornay sauce)

b) Hyphens

When two Christian names occur together in French it is usual practice to hyphenate them; this is not peculiar to menu French.

Crème Marie-Louise

Crème Marie-Rose

When a Christian name and a surname are used as a *dedication* then they are hyphenated:

Agnès Sorel (Person, 1422–1450)

Omelette Agnès-Sorel (Dedication)

Grimod de la Reynière (Person, 1758–1838)

Dartois Grimod-de-la-Reynière (Dedication)

(Further examples of the use of hyphens are given in Part Two, Section 5.)

c) Capitalisation and hyphenation

A further difference between French and English needs to be borne in mind in the writing of menu French. In English, titles are written with a capital letter (e.g.,

General, Doctor, Saint), whereas in French they are written with a small letter (le général, le docteur, le saint). However, when such titles are used in the dedication of a dish (or any other item such as, for example, a street) *two* changes take place: the title takes a capital letter and the name is hyphenated.

    Avenue Général-Leclerc

    Avenue Mont-Blanc

    Rue Saint-Joseph

Thus the English sentence 'General Leclerc was walking down the Avenue General Leclerc' would be rendered in French by 'Le général Leclerc descendait l'avenue Général-Leclerc.' (Note the use of small and capital letters and hyphens.) Examples of these changes occurring in menu French are:

    Mont-Blanc aux marrons (Mountain: 'le mont Blanc')

    Filet de boeuf Prince-Albert (Person: 'le prince Albert')

    Crème Saint-Germain (Person: 'le saint Germain')

d) Accents and the cedilla

i. There are three accents in French – the acute, the grave and the circumflex. They occur only over vowels, never over consonants. It is useful to remember the following points:

> the vowel –e– is the only one that can take all three accents;
> the letter –a– can take either the grave or the circumflex, never the acute;
> the letters –o–, –i–, –u– can only take the circumflex. (The letter –u– can in fact also take a grave accent, but this has no relevance to menu French.)

ii. It will be seen from the study of any modern example of French printing that the tendency is to omit all accents from capital letters.

iii. The cedilla is used only under the letter –c–. Its function is to keep the –c– soft (that is, with the sound 's' as opposed to the sound 'k'). Since –c– is always pronounced like an 's' before –e– or –i– then it can never take a cedilla when followed by these vowels. It will therefore only occur when the –c– is followed by –a–, –o–, or –u–. Of course, the fact that –c– is followed by –a–, –o– or –u– does not mean that it *must* take a cedilla, for it could be representing the sound 'k' not 's'. The capital C, unlike other capital letters, still takes a cedilla when pronounced as an –s–.
Examples:

> Dugléré (acute accents)
> Belle-Hélène (acute followed by a grave accent)
> Côtelette (circumflex accent)
> Canapé (C pronounced as 'k')
> provençale (c pronounced as 's')

iv. The *tréma* is used to separate the pronunciation of two vowels that would normally be pronounced together. The name 'Aida' would be pronounced as in English 'Ada' (approximate pronunciation); however, with the *tréma* over the –i–, it would be pronounced 'Ah-ee-da' (approximate pronunciation). Further examples, with *approximate* pronunciations are:

> Esaü ('Ay-z-ah-u')
> Héloïse ('Ay-lo-eez')
> Moïna ('Mo-ee-nah')
> Noël ('No-el')
> Raphaël ('Raff-ah-el')

Very occasionally the *tréma* is used without any resulting change occurring in the pronunciation (e.g., 'Saint-Saëns').

6. Foreign words

a) A number of words foreign to French often occur in menu French. As is to be expected, particularly in the case of words from languages that do not use the Roman alphabet, there are variations in the spelling of such words:

> cari, carri, currie, kari
> cola, kola
> Demidoff, Demidov
> goulache, goulasch, gulyas
> kougelhof, kouglof, kugelhopf
> pilaf, pilau, pilaw
> pouding, pudding
> quiche, kiche
> Romanoff, Romanov
> yaourt, yoghourt

b) Italian words in French

i. Italian words cause a little difficulty. Words such as cannelloni, ravioli, scampi, spaghetti, vermicelli are Italian plurals and should never, therefore, be given a final –s. If an adjective is used with such nouns, it is generally (and correctly)put into the plural:

> Scampi frits

Often, however, the words do tend to be used in French as collective nouns and are counted as singular:

> le macaroni   (Italian: i maccheroni)
> le vermicelle   (Italian: i vermicelli)

and so one finds:

> Consommé *au* macaroni
> Consommé *au* vermicelle

The word 'ravioli' tends to be regarded as plural:

> Consommé *aux* ravioli

ii. A few words need to be said about the adjectives that accompany these Italian words. If the menu is in French, then one ought to be consistent and put the adjective in French also:

        Spaghetti à la bolonaise

        Spaghetti à la napolitaine

The forms:

        Gnocchi alla romana

        Macaroni italiana (a mixture of French and Italian)

        Spaghetti bolognese

are Italian and should be reserved for the Italian menu. The word 'bolognaise' is a hybrid and is incorrect both in French and Italian.

7. Elision and liaison

a) The final –e of 'le' and 'de' is *elided* before another vowel or 'mute h':

        à le + ananas   becomes à l'ananas

        à le + oignon   becomes à l'oignon

b) The final –a of 'la' is elided before another vowel or mute 'h':

        à la + allemande   becomes à l'allemande

        à la + huile   becomes à l'huile

        à la + orange   becomes à l'orange

c) The final –s of 'les' and 'des' and the final –x of 'aux' are *pronounced* as a 'z' before a vowel or a mute 'h'. This is called 'liaison'.

> au*x* anchois   (–x pronounced as –z)
> le*s* oeufs   (–s pronounced as –z)
> le*s* oranges   (–s pronounced as –z)
> de*s* huîtres   (–s pronounced as –z)

There are, however, a number of words in French which begin with a vowel or with the letter 'h'– and before which the vowel is not elided or the final –s or –x pronounced in liaison:

> les hors-d'oeuvre
> à la Orly

(See p.51 for a list of such words occurring most commonly in menu French.)

8. The date

a) Days of the week are written with a small letter in French:

Monday	lundi	Friday	vendredi
Tuesday	mardi	Saturday	samedi
Wednesday	mercredi	Sunday	dimanche
Thursday	jeudi		

b) Months of the year are written with small letters in French:

January	janvier	July	juillet
February	février	August	août
March	mars	September	septembre
April	avril	October	octobre
May	mai	November	novembre
June	juin	December	décembre

c) The usual way of writing the date on the menu would be for example:

> Mercredi, 6 juillet 1977

N.B. The capital 'M' for the first letter of the line. Just the cardinal number is used, except for the first day of the month which would be abbreviated to '1er'.

d) The complete list of numbers from 1–31 may prove useful to those who wish to write the date out in full:

1st	le premier	12th	le douze	23rd	le vingt-trois
2nd	le deux	13th	le treize	24th	le vingt-quatre
3rd	le trois	14th	le quatorze	25th	le vingt-cinq
4th	le quatre	15th	le quinze	26th	le vingt-six
5th	le cinq	16th	le seize	27th	le vingt-sept
6th	le six	17th	le dix-sept	28th	le vingt-huit
7th	le sept	18th	le dix-huit	29th	le vingt-neuf
8th	le huit	19th	le dix-neuf	30th	le trente
9th	le neuf	20th	le vingt	31st	le trente et un
10th	le dix	21st	le vingt et un		
11th	le onze	22nd	le vingt-deux		

e) When the date is written in full one of the following forms is used:

Le mercredi, six juillet 1977

Mercredi, le six juillet 1977

Perhaps the former is the more usual.

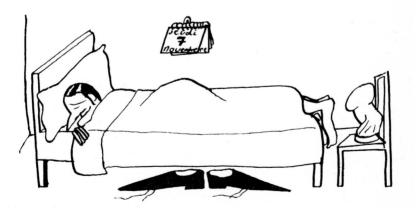

PART TWO

LISTS OF WORDS AND EXPRESSIONS
FREQUENTLY
USED IN MENU FRENCH

1. Frequently used adjectives with their forms and meanings

The following words are adjectives and change their form according to the noun they qualify, for example:

Bar *frit*	(masculine singular)
Truite de rivière *frite*	(feminine singular)
Harengs *frits*	(masculine plural)
Pommes *frites*	(feminine plural)

assorted	*scrambled*	*crystallised*
assorti	brouillé	cristallisé
assortie	brouillée	cristallisée
assortis	brouillés	cristallisés
assorties	brouillées	cristallisées

white	*warm*	*cooked*
blanc	chaud	cuit
blanche	chaude	cuite
blancs	chauds	cuits
blanches	chaudes	cuites

boiled	*coarsely broken up*	*devilled*
bouilli	concassé	diablé
bouillie	concassée	diablée
bouillis	concassés	diablés
bouillies	concassées	diablées

braised	*preserved*	*golden, glazed*
braisé	confit	doré
braisée	confite	dorée
braisés	confits	dorés
braisées	confites	dorées

sweet	*melted*	*smoked*
doux	fondu	fumé
douce	fondue	fumée
doux	fondus	fumés
douces	fondues	fumées
stuffed	*filled*	*garnished*
étoffé	fourré	garni
étoffée	fourrée	garnie
étoffés	fourrés	garnis
étoffées	fourrées	garnies
stewed	*fresh, cool*	*iced, glazed*
étuvé	frais	glacé
étuvée	fraîche	glacée
étuvés	frais	glacés
étuvées	fraîches	glacées
stuffed	*chilled, on ice*	*gratinated*
farci	frappé	gratiné
farcie	frappée	gratinée
farcis	frappés	gratinés
farcies	frappées	gratinées
flaming	*fried*	*grilled*
flambé	frit	grillé
flambée	frite	grillée
flambés	frits	grillés
flambées	frites	grillées
melting	*cold*	*chopped up, hashed*
fondant	froid	haché
fondante	froide	hachée
fondants	froids	hachés
fondantes	froides	hachées

marinaded
mariné
marinée
marinés
marinées

breadcrumbed
pané
panée
panés
panées

flavoured with 'pralin'
praliné
pralinée
pralinés
pralinées

decorated with meringue
meringué
meringuée
meringués
meringuées

sprinkled with parsley
persillé
persillée
persillés
persillées

of the spring
printanier
printanière
printaniers
printanières

small, delicate
mignon
mignonne
mignons
mignonnes

small, little
petit
petite
petits
petites

chilled, iced
rafraîchi
rafraîchie
rafraîchis
rafraîchies

moulded
moulé
moulée
moulés
moulées

flat
plat
plate
plats
plates

grated
râpé
râpée
râpés
râpées

black
noir
noire
noirs
noires

poached
poché
pochée
pochés
pochées

browned
rissolé
rissolée
rissolés
rissolées

mixed (in colour)
panaché
panachée
panachés
panachées

lightly braised
poêlé
poêlée
poêlés
poêlées

pink
rose
rose
roses
roses

roasted	*dry, dried*	*with chopped onion*
rôti	sec	soubisé
rôtie	sèche	soubisée
rôtis	secs	soubisés
rôties	sèches	soubisées
ribboned		*light and frothy*
rubané		soufflé
rubanée		soufflée
rubanés		soufflés
rubanées		soufflées
salted		*truffled*
salé		truffé
salée		truffée
salés		truffés
salées		truffées
salmon-coloured		*flavoured with vanilla*
saumoné		vanillé
saumonée		vanillée
saumonés		vanillés
saumonées		vanillées
tossed, sauté		*varied, various*
sauté		varié
sautée		variée
sautés		variés
sautées		variées
wild, uncultivated		*green*
sauvage		vert
sauvage		verte
sauvages		verts
sauvages		vertes

2. Proper nouns occurring in menu French

These words must always be spelled with a capital letter. Only unusual names of towns and countries are included. These place-names are given in italics, although often they are part of a person's title, e.g., Louis-Gabriel Suchet, Duc d'*Albuféra*.

Aboukir (Abukir)
Abrantès
Adrienne
Agnès-Sorel
Ahmed (Achmet)
Aïda
Aiglon
Aigrefeuille
Ajaccio
Aladin
Alaska
Albemarle
Albignac
Albina
Albion
Albuféra
Alexandra
Alhambra
Ali-Bab
Alice
Ali-Pache (Pacha, Pasha)
Alma
Alphonse XIII
Amélie
Amphitryon
André-Theuriet
Anna
Annette

Antin
Antoinette
Apicius
Archiduc-Salvator
Arenberg
Argenteuil
Arlequin
Armenonville
Arnold-Bennett
Auber
Augier
Aumale
Aurore

Babinski
Bachaumont
Bagration
Balmoral
Balue
Balzac
Banville
Baron-Brisse
Bayard
Béatrix
Beaugency
Beauharnais
Beaulieu
Beaumont

Beauvilliers
Belle-Angevine
Belle-Hélène
Belle-Meunière
Bellevue
Benoît
Benoîton
Béranger
Berchoux
Bercy
Berlioz
Bernis
Bignon
Biron
Bismarck
Bizet
Boieldieu
Boitelle
Boivin
Bonaparte
Bonvalet
Boris
Boston
Bourbon
Bourdaloue
Brancas
Brébant
Breteuil

Brillat-Savarin

Brimont

Brossard

Bugey

Cadmus

Caillou

Cambacérès

Cambyse

Camélia

Camérani

Capitole

Carême

Carignan

Carmen

Carnavalet

Carnot

Caroline

Caruso

Carvalho

Casanova

Casimir

Castelnaudary

Castiglione

Castile

Cavour

Célestine

Cellini

Cendrillon

Cérès

Chambéry

Chambord

Champollion

Champvallon

[1]*Chantilly*

[2]Chateaubriand

Chatouillard

Chauchat

Châtillon

Chaville

Chavillieu

Chénier

Chérubin

Chevreuse

Chiboust

Chimay

Chivry

Choisy

Choron

Christophe-Colomb

Clamart

Clarence

Claudine

Clermont

Clo-Clo

Clotilda

Cocherel

Colbert

Colette

Colnet

Comtesse-Marie

Comtesse-de-Riguidi

Condé

Conti

Coquelin

Coquibus

Crainquebille

Crapotte

Crécy

Crepazzi

Cubat

Cussy

Custine

Cyrano

Dalayrac

Dame-Blanche

Darblay

Daumet

Daudet

Daumont

Dauphiné

Déjazet

Delmonico

Demidov (Demidoff)

Diane

Dino

Doria

Dreux

Du Barry

Dubois

Du Bourg

Dugléré

[1]une chantilly = une crème Chantilly
[2]but un chateaubriand (the steak); note also the absence of the circumflex

Dumas
Durand
Duroc
Duxelles

Edna-May
Edouard VII
Edwin
Elisabeth
Elysée
Esaü
Eugénie
Excelsior

Fanchette
Fanchon
Fanchonnette
Faubonne
Favart
Feydeau
Figaro
Fleury
Florence
Florette
Florida
Fontanges
Fontenelle
Francillon
Frascati
Freneuse

Garfield
Garibaldi
Georgette

Georgia
Germaine
Germiny
Gismonda
Godard
Goubaud
Gouffé
Gramont
Grand-Veneur
Grimaldi
Grimod-de-la-Reynière

Halévy
Helder
Hélène
Héloïse
Henri-Duvernois
Henri IV
Henrietta
Héricart
Hermione
Holstein
Hortense
Hudson
Humbert
Humboldt

Impéria
Irène
Irma
Irving
Isabelle
Ivanhoé

Jackson
Jacquard
Jacqueline
Jacques
Jean-Bart
Jeanne-d'Arc
Jeannette
Jérôme
Jessica
Jockey-Club
Joinville
Joséphine
Jubilé
Judic
Jules-Janin
Julie
Julienne
Juliette-Récamier

Katoff
Kléber

Lady-Curzon
Lady-Egmont
Lafitte
Laguipière
Lamballe
Lambertye
La-Pérouse
La-Rochelle
Lathuile
La-Vallière
La-Varenne
Léopold

Lesseps
Levasseur
Lisette
London-House
Longchamp
Longueville
Lorenzo
Lorette
Louise
Louis-Forest
Louis XIV
Louis XV
Louis XVI
Louisette
Lucullus

Macaire
Madame-Récamier
Madeleine
Maeterlinck
Magenta
Magny
Maillot
Maire
Malakov (Malakoff)
Malmaison
Mancini
Manon
Marengo
Margot
Marguerite
Marguery
Marianne
Maria-Stella

Marie-Antoinette
Marie-Louise
Marie-Rose
Marie-Stuart
Marigny
Marivaux
Mascotte
Masséna
Massenet
Matignon
Maximilien
Médicis
Melba
Mercédès
Messine
Metternich
Meyerbeer
Mirabeau
Miramar
Mireille
Mirette
Mistral
Moïna
Monselet
Montaigne
Mont-Blanc
Mont-Bry
Mont-Dore
Monte-Carlo
Montesquieu
Montglas
Montgolfier
Montmorency
Montpensier

Montreuil
Montrouge
Morland
Mornay
Mourier
Murat

Nana
Nanette
Nantua
Nemours
Nemrod
Nesselrode
Néva
Newburg
Nichette
Ninon
Noailles
Noël
Novello

Océan
Odette
Offenbach
Orléans
Orlov (Orloff)
Orly
Opéra
Oudinot

Paillard
Palmyre
Parmentier
Parmentière

Pascal

Patti

Paul-Mounet

Pélissier

Pénélope

Pépita

Périgord

Périgueux

Périnette

Pernollet

Petit-Duc

Pierre-le-Grand

Pierrot

Pilleverjus

Pithiviers

Plombières

Pojarski

Polignac

Pompadour

Pont-Neuf

Port-Royal

Porte-Maillot

Prince-Albert

Prince-Orlov (Orloff)

Princesse-Alice

Printania

Quirinal

Rabelais

Rachel

Rambouillet

Raphaël

Réforme

Régence

Régina

Reine-Jeanne

Reine-Margot

Reine-Pédauque

Reine-de-Saba

Réjane

Renaissance

Riche

Richelieu

Riga

Rivière (Riviera)

Rivoli

Robert

Rohan

Romanov (Romanoff)

Rose-Marie

Rosière

Rossini

Rothomago

Rothschild

Rougemont

Rubens

Sagan

Saint-Cloud

Saint-Flour

Saint-Germain

Saint-Honoré

Saint-Hubert

Saint-Malo

Saint-Mars

Saint-Saëns

Sainte-Alliance

Sainte-Menehould

Sans-Gêne

Sarah-Bernhardt

Savary

Savoie

Serge

Sévigné

Singapour

Solférino

Sorges

Soubise

Souvarov (Souvaroff)

Stanley

Suchet

Sully

Suzette

Sylvette

Taillevent

Talleyrand

Talma

Tertillière

Tosca

Toscane

Tredern

Trianon

Trouville

Turbigo

Uzès

Valenciennes

Valençay

Valérien

Valéry	Victor-Hugo	Walewska
Valois	Victoria	*Washington*
Valromey	Villaret	Wladimir
Vatel	*Villars*	
Vauban	*Villeneuve*	Xavier
Verdier	Villeroi	
Véron	Visé	Yvette
Véronique	Voisin	
Vichy	Voltaire	
Victor-Emmanuel II		

3. Words and expressions never requiring capital letters

The masculine form of the adjective is given in brackets, though it is rarely needed in menu French. The English is a translation, not a description of the preparation which may vary from dish to dish. Where considered appropriate, an indication of the contents of the dish is given in brackets; for example, the translation of 'demi-deuil' is 'half-mourning' but 'with white sauce, cream and truffles' is more helpful.

à l'africaine	(africain)	in African style
à l'agenaise	(agenais)	in the style of Agen
à l'albigeoise	(albigeois)	in the style of Albi
à l'algérienne	(algérien)	in Algerian style
à l'allemande	(allemand)	in German style
à l'alsacienne	(alsacien)	in Alsatian style
ambassadeur, ambassadrice		Ambassador, Ambassadress
à l'américaine	(américain)	in American style
à l'amiral		in Admiral style
à l'ancienne	(ancien)	in old-fashioned style
à l'andalouse	(andalou)	in Andalusian style
à l'angevine	(angevin)	in the style of Anjou
à l'antiboise	(antibois)	in the style of Antibes
à l'anversoise	(anversois)	in the style of Antwerp
à l'archiduc		Archduke
à l'ardennaise	(ardennais)	in the Ardennes style
à l'ariégeoise	(ariégeois)	in the style of Ariège
à l'arlésienne	(arlésien)	in the style of Arles
à l'armoricaine	(armoricain)	in Breton style
à l'aurore		with an *aurore* sauce
à l'auvergnate	(auvergnat)	in the Auvergne style
à la bamboche		(fried salt-cod on bed of vegetables)
à la banquière		in banker's style
à la barigoule		(braised, stuffed artichokes)
bar-man		barman

à la basquaise	(basquais)	in the Basque style
à la batelière		in boatman style
à la bavaroise	(bavarois)	in Bavarian style
à la bayonnaise	(bayonnais)	in the style of Bayonne
à la béarnaise	(béarnais)	in the Béarn style
à la béchamel		with a Béchamel sauce
à la bellevilloise	(bellevillois)	in the style of Belleville
à la bénédictine		(a preparation of salt cod)
à la bernoise	(bernois)	in the style of Berne
à la berrichonne	(berrichon)	in the style of Berry
à la biarrotte	(biarrot)	in the style of Biarritz
à la bigarade		(with bitter orange sauce)
à la bigourdane	(bigourdan)	in the style of Bigorre
à la bohémienne	(bohémien)	in Bohemian style
à la bonne-femme		in housewife style
à la bolonaise	(bolonais)	in the style of Bologna
à la bordelaise	(bordelais)	in Bordeaux style
à la bostonnaise	(bostonnais)	in Boston style
à la bouchère		in butcher's style
à la boulangère		in baker's style
à la bouquetière		(vegetables arranged in 'bouquets')

à la bourbonnaise	(bourbonnais)	in the style of the Réunion Isle
à la bourgeoise		in plain style
à la bourguignonne	(bourguignon)	in Burgundy style
à la bretonne	(breton)	in Breton style
à la brunoise	(brunois)	in Brunoy style
à la bruxelloise	(bruxellois)	in the style of Brussels
à la brabançonne	(brabançon)	in Brabant style
à la brésilienne	(brésilien)	in Brazilian style
à la bûcheronne		in woodcutter's style
à la canadienne	(canadien)	in Canadian style
à la cancalaise	(cancalais)	in the style of Cancale
à la canotière		in boatman style
à la cantalienne	(cantalien)	in Cantal style
capucine		Capuchin nun
à la cardinal		(with a Cardinal sauce)
à la carmélite		in Carmelite (nun) style
à la catalane	(catalan)	in Catalonian style
à la cévenole	(cévenol)	in Cévennes style
à la chablaisienne	(chablaisien)	in the style of Chablais
à la châlonnaise	(châlonnais)	in the style of Châlon
à la champenoise	(champenois)	in Champagne style
à la chanoinesse		in the style of a canoness
à la charcutière		in pork butcher style
à la chasseur		with a *chasseur* sauce
à la châtelaine		in Lord of the Manor style
château		(olive-shaped potatoes, roasted)
à la chevalière		in horse-rider style
à la chilienne	(chilien)	in Chile style
à la chinonaise	(chinonais)	in the style of Chinon
à la chipolata		(with chipolata sausages)
commodore		Commodore
comtesse		Countess
à la comtoise	(comtois)	in the style of Franche-Comté

à la crapaudine		(chicken cut to look like toad)
à la créole	(créole)	in Creole style
à la cressonnière		(with water-cress)
cultivateur		farmer, horticulturist
czarine		Czarina
à la danoise	(danois)	in Danish style
à la dauphine		in Dauphiness style
à la dauphinoise	(dauphinois)	in the style of Dauphiné
demi-deuil		(with truffles, white sauce and cream)
à la diable		with a *diable* sauce
à la dieppoise	(dieppois)	in Dieppe style
à la dijonnaise	(dijonnais)	in Dijon style
à la diplomate		with a *diplomate* sauce
à la duchesse		in Duchess style
à la duxelles		(onions and mushrooms)
à l'écossaise	(écossais)	in Scottish style
à l'égyptienne	(égyptien)	in Egyptian style
à l'épicurienne		in Epicurean style
à l'espagnole	(espagnol)	in Spanish style
à la favorite		fit for the King's favourite
à la fécampoise	(fécampois)	in the style of Fécamp
à la fermière		in farmer style
à la financière		in financier style
à la flamande	(flamand)	in Flemish style
fleuriste		florist
à la florentine	(florentin)	in the style of Florence
à la forestière		in forester style
à la française	(français)	in French style
à la franco-américaine	(franco-américain)	in Franco-American style
à la fribourgeoise	(fribourgeois)	in the style of Freibourg

à la gasconne	(gascon)	in the style of Gascony
au gastronome		in gastronome style
à la gauloise	(gaulois)	in the style of Gaul
en gelée		(in jelly)
à la génoise	(génois)	in Genoese style
gentilhomme		nobleman
à la gourmande		(plentiful)
grand-duc		Grand Duke
à la grand-mère		in grandmother style
à la grecque	(grec)	in Greek style
à la grenobloise	(grenoblois)	in the style of Grenoble
à la hambourgeoise	(hambourgeois)	in Hamburg style
hérisson		(apples made to look like hedgehogs – stuck with almonds)
à la hollandaise	(hollandais)	in Dutch style
à la hongroise	(hongrois)	in Hungarian style
à l'hôtelière		in hotel-keeper's style
à la houblonnière		in hop-grower's style
à la hussarde		in hussar style
à l'impératrice		in Empress style
à l'impériale		in Imperial style
à l'indienne	(indien)	in Indian style
à l'infante		in Infanta style
à l'irlandaise	(irlandais)	in Irish style
à l'italienne	(italien)	in Italian style
à l'ivoire		(with an Ivory sauce)
à la japonaise	(japonais)	in Japanese style
à la jardinière		in gardener's style
à la juive	(juif)	in Jewish style
à la julienne		(with vegetables cut into thin strips)
à la jurassienne	(jurassien)	in the style of the Jura

à la landaise	(landais)	in the style of the Landes
à la languedocienne	(languedocien)	in the style of the Languedoc
à la liégeoise	(liégeois)	in the style of Liége
à la ligurienne	(ligurien)	in the style of Liguria
à la limousine	(limousin)	in the style of Limoges
à la lituanienne	(lituanien)	in Lithuanian style
à la livournaise	(livournais)	in the style of Livorno
à la livonienne	(livonien)	in the style of Livonia
à la lorraine	(lorrain)	in Lorraine style
à la lyonnaise	(lyonnais)	in the style of Lyon
à la macédoine		(with macédoine of vegetables)
à la mâconnaise	(mâconnais)	in the style of Mâcon
à la madrilène	(madrilène)	in the style of Madrid
maharadjah		Maharajah
à la maître d'hôtel		in Head waiter style
à la maltaise	(maltais)	in Maltese style
à la maraîchère		in market-gardener style
à la marchand de vins		in wine-seller style
à la maréchale		in marshal style
à la marinière		in mariner style
marquise		Marchioness
à la marseillaise	(marseillais)	in Marseille style
a la matelote		(poached in red wine)
à la ménagère		in housewife's style
à la mentonnaise	(mentonnais)	in the style of Menton
à la meunière		in the style of the miller
meurette		(preparation of stewed fish)
à la mexicaine	(mexicain)	in Mexican style
mikado		Mikado
à la milanaise	(milanais)	in the style of Milan
mimosa		mimosa
à la mirepoix		(with a mixture of vegetables)
au miroir		(baked egg with cream)

à la mode		(stewed beef)
à la moldave	(moldave)	in Moldavian style
à la moscovite	(moscovite)	in the style of Moscow
mousseline		(Hollandaise sauce with whipped cream)
à la moderne		in modern style
à la marocaine	(marocain)	in Moroccan style
à la nantaise	(nantais)	in the style of Nantes
à la nantuatienne	(nantuatien)	in the style of Nantua
à la napolitaine	(napolitain)	in the style of Naples
nature		natural, plainly cooked
négresse		negress
à la niçoise	(niçois)	in the style of Nice
à la nivernaise	(nivernais)	in Nivernais style
à la normande	(normand)	in Normandy style
à la norvégienne	(norvégien)	in Norwegian style
à l'occitane	(occitan)	in the style of Occitania
à l'occitanienne	(occitanien)	in the style of an Occitanian
à l'oranaise	(oranais)	in the style of Oran
à l'orientale	(oriental)	in Oriental style
à la panetière		(dressed in hollowed bread roll)
à la parisienne	(parisien)	in Parisian style
à la parmesane	(parmesan)	in the style of Parma
à la paysanne		in peasant style
à la pèlerine		in pilgrim style
à la périgourdine	(périgourdin)	in the style of Périgord
à la piémontaise	(piémontais)	in the style of Piedmont
à la poitevine	(poitevin)	in the style of Poitou
à la polonaise	(polonais)	in Polish style
à la portugaise	(portugais)	in Portuguese style
à la poulette		with an *allemande* sauce

à la princesse		in princess style
à la printanière	(printanier)	spring
à la provençale	(provençal)	in the style of Provence
à la ravigote		(with a type of *vinaigrette* sauce)
à la reine		in the style of a queen
à la romaine	(romain)	in Roman style
à la rouennaise	(rouennais)	in the style of Rouen
à la royale		in regal style
à la russe	(russe)	in Russian style

santé		health
à la sarde	(sarde)	in Sardinian style
à la sarladaise	(sarladais)	in the style of Sarlat
à la sarrasine	(sarrasin)	in Saracen style
à la savoyarde	(savoyard)	in the style of Savoy
saxon		Saxon
à la sibérienne	(sibérien)	in Siberian style
à la sicilienne	(sicilien)	in Sicilian style

à la soissonnaise	(soissonnais)	in the style of Soissons
à la strasbourgeoise	(strasbourgeois)	in the style of Strasbourg
à la suédoise	(suédois)	in Swedish style
à la suisse	(suisse)	in Swiss style
sultane		Sultana
sauce suprême		with a suprême sauce
surprise		surprise
à la tartare		with a Tartare sauce
à la tortue		(with a mixture of herbs)
à la toscane	(toscan)	in the style of Tuscany
à la toulonnaise	(toulonnais)	in the style of Toulon
à la tourangelle	(tourangeau)	in the style of Touraine
à la trouvillaise	(trouvillais)	in the style of Trouville
à la turque	(turc)	in Turkish style
à la tyrolienne	(tyrolien)	in the Tyrol style
tzarine		Czarina
à la valentinoise	(valentinois)	in the style of Valence
à la vauclusienne	(vauclusien)	in the style of Vaucluse
à la vendéenne	(vendéen)	in the style of Vendée
à la vénitienne	(vénitien)	in Venetian style
à la viennoise	(viennois)	in Viennese style, *or* in the style of Vienna
à la vigneronne		in vine-grower's style
à la villageoise		in villager's style
à la vinaigrette		(with a *vinaigrette* sauce)
à la vosgienne	(vosgien)	in the Vosges style
à la yorkaise	(yorkais)	in the style of York
à la zingara		in gypsy style

4. Expressions denoting methods of cooking, accompaniments and garnishes

These expressions should never be written with capital letters. Obvious accompaniments have been omitted, e.g., 'aux petits pois'. The meanings of most of these items can be ascertained from the vocabulary given in Part Four.

à l'aigre-doux
amandine
aux anchois
à l'armagnac
en aspic
à l'asti
en attereaux

en ballon
en ballotine
en beignets
en bellevue
au beurre
au beurre blanc
au beurre fondu
au beurre maître d'hôtel
au beurre noir
au beurre noisette
bitoke
au blanc
en blanquette
au bleu
en bordure
en bordure de riz
en boulettes
en branches
en brioche
à la broche

en brochettes
en buisson

en caisses
en caissettes
au calvados
à la canotière
au caramel
à la casserole
en casserole
en cassoulet
en cassoulettes
au chablis
au chambertin
au champagne
en chartreuse
en chaud-froid
en chausson
en chemise
à cheval
aux cheveux d'ange
en cheveux d'ange
en chevreuil
en chiffonnade
en civet
au claret
en cocotte
en compote

à la coque
en coquilles
en cornets
en côtelettes
en couronne
au court-bouillon
à la crème
en crépine
en crépinettes
au cresson alénois
aux crevettes
en cromesquis
à la croque-au-sel
en croûte(s)
aux croûtons
à la cuiller
au curaçao
au currie

en daube
aux diablotins
en douillon

à l'eau-de-vie
à l'écarlate
en épigrammes
en escabèche
en estouffade

à la fine champagne
à la flip
au fondant
au four
à la frangipane
en fricassée
en fritot
au fromage
au frontignan
au fumet

en gélatine
garbure
en gâteau
à la gelée
en gibelotte
au gras
au gratin
au gril
au gruyère

au homard
à l'huile

en julienne
au jus
au kirsch
au kola

au lambic
au lard maigre
en lorgnette

au macaroni

au madère
au maigre
au marsala
en matelote
à la mayonnaise
en mayonnaise
à la minute
miroton

à la nage
au naturel
à la neige
au nid
aux nouilles

aux oeufs durs
en omelette
à l'orange
à l'oseille

au pain
en pain
en pantin
au paprika
au parfait amour
au parmesan
en pâte
en paupiettes
au persil
en petits pois
en pilaf
au pissalat
à la pistache
en pistache

au plat
à la poêle
poivrade
en portefeuille
au porto
au pot
en potée
en pouding
en poupeton
au praliné
à la presse
en purée
à la purée de légumes

en quenelles

en rabotte
au rhum
au riz
au riz pilaf
en robe de chambre
en robe des champs
au roquefort

en salade
en salmis
au salpicon de homard
au salpicon de langouste
en sauce
en sauce tomate
en soufflé
sous la cendre
sous les cendres
au sucre

sur canapés   en terrine   au vert
sur chicorée   en torsade   au vert-pré
sur croûtons   en tortue   au vinaigre
sur gazon   en tranches   à la vinaigrette
sur le gril   aux truffes   au vin blanc
sur le plat   au vin rouge
sur purée de champignons   à la vapeur   en volute
en surprise   au velouté
                        au verjus   au xérès
en tapioca   au vermicelle

5. Miscellaneous lists

a) The following are to be noted for their hyphens.

aigre-doux	contre-filet	gras-double
bar-man	(plural: contre-filets)	hors-d'oeuvre
Belle-Meunière	court-bouillon	mange-tout
bonne-femme	croûte-au-pot	mardi-gras
céleri-rave	Dame-Blanche	petit-duc
(plural: céleris-raves)	demi-deuil	[1]pieds-de-mouton
chaud-froid	demi-pamplemousse	pot-au-feu
chou-fleur	demi-perdreau	pré-salé
(plural: choux-fleurs)	eau-de-vie	tutti-frutti
chou-rave	franco-américaine	vert-pré
(plural: choux-raves)	grand-duc	vol-au-vent
	grand-mère	

[1] A kind of mushroom. 'Pieds de mouton' (without hyphens) would mean 'sheep's trotters'.

b) Note the lack of elision (and, in pronunciation, the lack of liaison) in the following.

au hachis	aux haricots	à la hollandaise
au haddock	(–x is not pronounced)	au homard
le halicot	en hérisson	à la hongroise
à la hambourgeoise	(–n is not pronounced)	les hors-d'oeuvre
aux harengs	en hochepot	(–s is not pronounced)
(–x is not pronounced)	(–n is not pronounced)	à la hussarde

c) 'à la mode' is rarely used in menu items; it has survived in these few expressions.

à la mode	à la mode de Bugey	à la mode de Sorges
(in Boeuf à la mode)	à la mode de Cocherel	à la mode de Visé
à la mode béarnaise	à la mode des mariniers	

PART THREE

EXAMPLES OF MENU ITEMS

Note: These examples are arranged alphabetically according to the *preparation*, not according to the initial letter of the *item*.

Bombe *Aboukir*

Tournedos *Abrantès*

Sole *Adrienne*

Selle d'agneau *à l'africaine*

Oeufs *à l'agenaise*

Tartelettes *Agnès-Sorel*

Tournedos *Ahmed*

Turbot *Aïda*

Ris de veau *l'Aiglon*

Coupe *à l'aigre-doux*

Oeufs mignons *d'Aigrefeuille*

Consommé *Ajaccio*

Oeufs *Aladin*

Omelette soufflée *Alaska*

Sole *Albemarle*

Salade *d'Albignac*

Omelette *Albina*

Consommé *Albion*

Poularde *Albuféra*

Noisettes d'agneau *Alexandra*

Tournedos *à l'algérienne*

Glace *Alhambra*

Salade *Ali-Bab*

Salade *Alice*

Consommé *Ali-Pache*

Choucroute en salade *à l'allemande*

Salade *Alma*

Sole *Alphonse XIII*

Oie *à l'alsacienne*

Tartelettes *amandines*

Suprêmes de volailles *ambassadeur*

Potage *Ambassadeurs*

Consommé *ambassadrice*

Oeufs *Amélia*

Barbue *à l'américaine*

Sole *à l'amiral*

Poulet *Amphitryon*

Croûtes *aux anchois*

Carpe farcie *à l'ancienne*

Poularde *à l'andalouse*

Omelette *André-Theuriet*

Roulade d'anguille *à l'angevine*

Ragoût d'agneau *à l'anglaise*

Baron de mouton aux pommes *Anna*

Poulet sauté *Annette*

Sardines *à l'antiboise*

Suprêmes de barbue *D'Antin*

Pouding *Antoinette*

Ris de veau *à l'anversoise*

Oeufs *Apicius*

Poulet sauté *archiduc*

Poulet sauté *Archiduc-Salvator*

Pâté chaud de grives *à l'ardennaise*

Pouding *Aremberg*

Oeufs brouillés *Argenteuil*

Poitrine de mouton farcie *à l'ariégeoise*

Charlotte *Arlequin*

Sole *à l'arlésienne*

Bécasse à *l'armagnac*

Noisettes d'agneau *Armenonville*

Filets de sole à *l'armoricaine*

Omelette *Arnold-Bennett*

Pommes *en aspic*
Sabayon à *l'asti*
Ris de veau *en attereaux*
Oeufs *Auber*
Oeufs *Augier*
Sole *Aumale*
Pommes *Aurore*
Petits soufflés à *l'aurore*
Tarte à *l'autrichienne*
Queue de boeuf à *l'auvergnate*

Oeufs *Babinski*
Oeufs *Bachaumont*
Barquettes *Bagration*
Epaule de mouton *en ballon*
Chou vert farci *en ballotine*
Oeufs *Balmoral*
Pommes *Balue*
Oeufs brouillés *Balzac*
Morue à *la bamboche*
Poularde à *la banquière*
Oeufs *Banville*
Artichauts à *la barigoule*
Côtelettes d'agneau *bar-man*
Artichauts *Baron-Brisse*
Confit d'oie à *la basquaise*
Filets de sole à *la batelière*
Ananas à *la bavaroise*
Poulet sauté *Bayard*
Canapés à *la bayonnaise*
Pot-au-feu à *la béarnaise*
Noisettes d'agneau *Béatrix*
Tournedos *Beaugency*
Carré d'agneau *Beauharnais*

Suprêmes de volaille *Beaulieu*
Oeufs *Beaumont*
Croûtes aux bananes *à la Beauvilliers*
Clams *en beignets*
Salsifis à *la béchamel*
Poires *Belle-Angevine* glacées
Oeufs *Belle-Hélène*
Truite de rivière *Belle-Meunière*
Oeufs à *la bellevilloise*
Côte de veau *Bellevue*
Dinde en galantine *en bellevue*
Morue à *la bénédictine*
Filets de brochet *Benoît*
Morue *Benoîton*
Oeufs *Béranger*
Truite saumonée *Berchoux*
Foie de veau *Bercy*
Barbue à *la sauce Bercy*
Oeufs *Berlioz*
Oeufs *Bernis*
Pommes à *la berrichonne*
Courgettes pochées *au beurre*
Brochet *au beurre blanc*
Merlan bouilli *au beurre fondu*
Chateaubriand grillé *au beurre maître
    d'hôtel*
Endives *au beurre noir*
Morue *au beurre noisette*
Poulet sauté à *la biarrotte*
Filets de canard à *la bigarade*
Sole *Bignon*
Omelette à *la bigourdane*
Sole *Biron*
Tournedos de boeuf *Bismarck*

Bifteck *bitoke*
Consommé *Bizet*
Bettes *au blanc*
Champignons *en blanquette*
Truite vivante *au bleu*
Faisan *à la bohémienne*
Crème *Boieldieu*
Filets de sole *Boitelle*
Poulet sauté *Boivin*
Spaghetti *à la bolonaise*
Oeufs pochés *Bombay*
Sole *Bonaparte*
Ragoût d'oie *à la bonne-femme*
Oeufs *Bonvalet*
Rognons de veau *à la bordelaise*
Hachis de boeuf *en bordure*
Cailles à la financière *en bordure de riz*
Filets d'esturgeon *Boris*
Potage *Boston*
Saumon fumé *à la bostonnaise*
Côtelettes de mouton *à la bouchère*
Pommes *à la boulangère*
Boeuf *en boulettes*
Maquereau *à la boulonnaise*
Baron de mouton *à la bouquetière*
Poularde de riz *Bourbon*
Ananas glacé *à la bourbonnaise*
Abricots *Bourdaloue*
Ragoût de boeuf *à la bourgeoise*
Oie *à la bourguignonne*
Tournedos *à la brabançonne*
Escalope de veau *Brancas*
Céleris *en branches*
Tournedos de boeuf *Brébant*

Filets de sole *Breteuil*
Limande *à la bretonne*
Bécasse sautée *Brillat-Savarin*
Timbale de ris d'agneau *Brimont*
Foie gras *en brioche*
Poularde de Surrey *à la broche*
Foie de veau *en brochettes*
Côtelettes d'agneau *Brossard*
Purée Conti *à la brunoise*
Omelette *à la bruxelloise*
Demi-perdreau en cocotte *à la bûcheronne*
Brochet rôti *à la mode de Bugey*
Blanchailles *en buisson*

Bombe *Cadmus*
Tête de veau *Caillou*
Cailles *en caisses*
Oeufs *en caissettes*
Bécasse *au calvados*
Escalopes de foie gras *Cambacérès*
Bombe *Cambyse*
Crème *Camélia*
Charlotte *Camérani*
Saumon *à la canadienne*
Merlan *à la cancalaise*
Matelote d'anguille *à la canotière*
Pommes *à la cantalienne*
Poulet *en capilotade*
Oie en daube *Capitole*
Pouding glacé *capucine*
Abricots à l'eau-de-vie *au caramel*
Ragoût de homard *à la cardinal*
Beignets d'ananas *à la Carême*
Noisettes d'agneau *Carignan*

Cromesquis *à la carmélite*
Crème *Carmen*
Oeufs *Carnavalet*
Bombe *Carnot*
Crème *Caroline*
Spaghetti *Caruso*
Rognons de mouton *Carvalho*
Salade *Casanova*
Escalopes de veau *Casimir*
Rôti de boeuf *à la casserole*
Rognons de veau *en casserole*
Oeufs *en cassolettes*
Haricots blancs frais *en cassoulet*
Cassoulet de *Castelnaudary*
Filets de sole *Castiglione*
Brochet *Castile*
Epaule d'agneau *à la catalane*
Fonds d'artichauts *Cavour*
Consommé *Célestine*
Consommé *Cellini*
Crépinettes *Cendrillon*
Crème *Cérès*
Coupe glacée *à la cévenole*
Escargots *à la chablaisienne*
Moules *au chablis*
Anguille *au vin de Chablis* en gelée
Rissoles *à la chalonnaise*
Râble de lièvre *au chambertin*
Omelette *Chambéry*
Darne de saumon *Chambord*
Truite saumonée froide *au champagne*
Saumon glacé *à la champenoise*
Rognons de mouton sautés *aux champignons*

Côtelettes de mouton *Champollion*
Côtelette d'agneau *Champvallon*
Soufflé de cervelle *à la chanoinesse*
Ananas glacé *à la chantilly*
Bordure de poires *Chantilly*
Haricots blancs secs *à la charcutière*
Oeufs *Chartres*
Timbale *en chartreuse*
Oeufs *à la chasseur*
Pommes *château*
Bombe *Chateaubriand*
Omelette *à la châtelaine*
Oeufs brouillés *Châtillon*
Pommes frites *Chatouillard*
Filets de sole *Chauchat*
Côte de veau *en chaud-froid*
Jambon *en chausson*
Oeufs *Chaville*
Timbales de queues d'écrevisses *Chavillieu*
Caneton rouennais *en chemise*
Oeufs *Chénier*
Barbue *Chérubin*
Clams *à cheval*
Poularde *à la chevalière*
Consommé *aux cheveux d'ange*
Carottes *en cheveux d'ange*
Filet mignon de mouton *en chevreuil*
Oeufs *Chevreuse*
Cornets *Chiboust*
Laitues *en chiffonnade*
Consommé *à la chilienne*
Oeufs *Chimay*
Ragoût de dindonneau *à la chipolata*

Filets de sole *Chivry*
Côtelettes de mouton *Choiseul*
Omelette *Choisy*
Tournedos *Choron*
Consommé *Christophe-Colomb*
Lapin *en civet*
Baron d'agneau *Clamart*
Oeufs *Clarence*
Cerises *au claret*
Alose *Claudine*
Pouding *Clermont*
Coupe *Clo-Clo*
Consommé *Clotilda*
Alose étoffée *à la mode de Cocherel*
Carré d'agneau *en cocotte*
Coquilles Saint-Jacques frites *Colbert*
Gâteau *Colette*
Consommé *Colnet*
Consommé *commodore*
Abricots *en compote*
Oeufs *comtesse*
Biscuit *Comtesse-Marie*
Escargots *Comtesse-de-Riguidi*
Poularde *à la comtoise*
Cerises *Condé*
Côtelette de chevreuil *Conti*
Oeuf *à la coque*
Bombe *Coquelin*
Lapin *Coquibus*
Laitances *en coquilles à la normande*
Oeufs *en côtelettes*
Brioche *en couronne*
Thon *au court-bouillon*
Pommes *Crainquebille*

Pigeonneau *à la crapaudine*
Coupe glacée *Crapotte*
Bouchées *Crécy*
Homard *à la crème*
Rissoles *à la créole*
Perdreau *en crépine* Brillat-Savarin
Langues de mouton *en crépinettes*
Beignets *Crepazzi*
Consommé *au cresson alénois*
Salade au céleri-rave *à la cressonnière*
Oeufs brouillés *aux crevettes*
Oeufs *en cromesquis*
Fèves *à la croque-au-sel*
Macaroni *en croquettes*
Mauviettes *en croûte*
Consommé *croûte-au-pot*
Omelette *aux croûtons*
Filets de sole *Cubat*
Gigot de mouton *à la cuiller*
Potage *cultivateur*
Crème à l'anglaise *au curaçao*
Lapin sauté *au currie*
Côte de veau *Cussy*
Côte de veau *Custine*
Bombe *Cyrano*
Omelette *czarine*

Consommé *Dalayrac*
Bombe *Dame-Blanche*
Flan de cerises *à la danoise*
Potage *Darblay*
Caneton *en daube* à la gelée
Oeufs *Daudet*
Consommé *Daumet*

Filets de sole *Daumont*
Rissoles *à la dauphine*
Croquettes de pommes de terre *Dauphiné*
Gratin *à la dauphinoise*
Filets de sole *Déjazet*
Homard *Delmonico*
Poularde *demi-deuil*
Ballotine de poularde *Demidov*
Poularde *Derby*
Harengs grillés *à la diable*
Consommé *aux diablotins*
Bécasse *Diane*
Filets de maquereaux *à la dieppoise*
Omelette *à la dijonnaise*
Oeufs *Dino*
Filets de sole *à la diplomate*
Poularde *Doria*
Poires *en douillon*
Côte de veau *Dreux*
Carré d'agneau *Du Barry*
Sole *Dubois*
Pommes *Du Bourg*
Cailles grillées *à la duchesse*
Filet de turbot *à la Dugléré*
Noisettes de boeuf *Dumas*
Poulet sauté *Durand*
Filet mignon *Duroc*
Filets de barbue *à la duxelles*

Cerises *à l'eau-de-vie*
Velouté de volaille *à l'écossaise*
Oeufs *à l'écarlate*
Coupe *Edna-May*
Consommé *Edouard VII*

Pêches *Edwin*
Crème *à l'égyptienne*
Pommes *Elisabeth*
Tournedos *Elysée*
Timbales *à l'épicurienne*
Poitrine d'agneau *en épigrammes*
Crème *Esaü*
Morue *en escabèche*
Ballotine de poularde *à l'espagnole*
Perdreau *en estouffade*
Bombe *Eugénie*
Biscuit glacé *Excelsior*

Gâteau *Fanchette*
Mousse *Fanchon*
Bouchées *Fanchonnette*
Potage *Faubonne*
Oeufs *Favart*
Filets de sole *à la fécampoise*
Rissoles *à la fermière*
Omelette *Feydeau*
Pommes *Figaro*
Ris de veau *à la financière*
Fraises *à la fine champagne*
Hochepot *à la flamande*
Langue de boeuf braisée *fleuriste*
Consommé *Fleury*
Consommé *à la flip*
Consommé *Florence*
Coquilles de saumon *à la florentine*
Consommé *Florette*
Cocktail *Florida*
Glace *au fondant*
Potage *Fontanges*

Asperges *Fontenelle*
Perdreau *à la forestière*
Petits pois *à la française*
Salade *Francillon*
Homard *à la franco-américaine*
Choux *à la frangipane*
Contre-filet *Frascati*
Epaule d'agneau *Freneuse*
Bitoke de veau *à la fribourgeoise*
Lapin *en fricassée*
Langues de mouton *en fritot*
Canapés *au fromage de Gruyère*
Melon rafraîchi *au frontignan*
Bécasse *au fumet*

Dinde *en galantine* en bellevue
Potage *garbure*
Oeufs *Garfield*
Consommé *Garibaldi*
Epaule d'agneau *à la gasconne*
Petits pâtés *au gastronome*
Foie de veau *en gâteau*
Ballotine d'anguille *à la gauloise*
Aloyau braisé *à la gelée*
Anguille au vin de Chablis *en gelée*
Potage *gentilhomme*
Oeufs brouillés *Georgette*
Consommé *Georgia*
Consommé *Germaine*
Potage *Germiny*
Lapin *en gibelotte*
Bombe *Gismonda*
Ballotine de poularde *Godard*
Brioche *Goubaud*

Tournedos *à la Gouffé*
Cailles *à la gourmande*
Consommé *Gramont*
Dinde étoffée *grand-duc*
Poulet en cocotte *grand-mère*
Rognon de veau émincé *Grand-Veneur*
Potage Bagration *au gras*
Aubergines *au gratin*
Quartiers d'artichauts *à la grecque*
Truite de torrent *à la grenobloise*
Côtelettes de mouton *au gril*
Flétan *Grimaldi*
Côte de veau hachée *Grimod-de-la-Reynière*
Rissoles *au gruyère*

Oeufs *Halévy*
Bifteck *à la hambourgeoise*
Tournedos *Helder*
Rocher *Hélène*
Suprême de barbue *Héloïse*
Homard *Henri-Duvernois*
Tournedos *Henri IV*
Salade *Henrietta*
Bombe *Héricart*
Pommes *en hérisson*
Poulet sauté *Hermione*
Cabillaud *à la hollandaise*
Escalopes de veau *Holstein*
Omelette *au homard*
Champignons *à la hongroise*
Crème *Hortense*
Truite de rivière *à l' hôtelière*
Consommé *à la houblonnière*

Consommé *Hudson*
Pommes *à l'huile*
Oeufs *Humbert*
Crème *Humboldt*
Truite de rivière *à la hussarde*

Bombe *impératrice*
Salade *Impéria*
Riz *à l'impératrice*
Paupiettes de saumon *à l'impériale*
Darne de cabillaud *à l'indienne*
Consommé *à l'infante*
Poire *Irène*
Ragoût *à l'irlandaise*
Salade *Irma*
Timbale *Irving*
Vol-au-vent *Isabelle*
Quartiers d'artichauts *à l'italienne*
Croûte *Ivanhoé*
Ris de veau *à l'ivoire*

Pommes *Jackson*
Poulet sauté *Jacquard*
Potage *Jacqueline*
Filets de sole *Jacques*
Tartelettes *à la japonaise*
Ris de veau *à la jardinière*
Croquettes *Jean-Bart*
Fraises *Jeanne-d'Arc*
Suprêmes de volaille *Jeannette*
Oeufs *Jérôme*
Omelette *Jessica*
Oeufs *Jockey-Club*
Filets de sole *Joinville*

Poulet sauté *Joséphine*
Crème *Jubilé*
Consommé *Judic*
Tournedos sauté *Jules-Janin*
Crème *Julie*
Consommé *Julienne*
Flan au fromage *Juliette-Récamier*
Carpe *à la juive*
Purée Conti *à la julienne*
Omelette *à la jurassienne*
Macaroni *au jus*

Poulet *Katoff*
Fruits rafraîchis *au kirsch*
Filets de turbot *Kléber*
Crème *à la kola*

Poulet *Lady-Curzon*
Sole *Lady-Egmont*
Poulet sauté *Lafitte*
Dartois *Laguipière*
Cailles en caisses *Lamballe*
Caneton de Rouen *Lambertye*
Carbonnades *au lambic*
Pommes *à la landaise*
Aubergines au gratin *à la languedocienne*
Poulet sauté *La-Pérouse*
Oeufs brouillés *au lard maigre*
Poulet de grain sauté *Lathuile*
Omelette *La-Vallière*
Côtelettes de mouton *La-Varenne*
Consommé *Léopold*
Consommé *Lesseps*
Filets mignons *Levasseur*

Consommé *Leverrier*
Rognons de veau *à la liégeoise*
Pannequets *à la ligurienne*
Carré de porc *à la limousine*
Salade *Lisette*
Ravioli *à la lituanienne*
Rouget *à la livournaise*
Harengs *à la livonienne*
Filet de boeuf *London-House*
Potage *Longchamp*
Potage *Longueville*
Salade *Lorenzo*
Pommes *Lorette*
Merlan *en lorgnette*
Prunes flambées *à la lorraine*
Suprêmes de sole *Louise*
Gratin de reinette *Louisette*
Omelette *Louis-Forest*
Filet de boeuf *Louis XIV*
Poulet sauté *Louis XV*
Noisettes *Louis XVI*
Filets de lièvre *Lucullus*
Haricots verts *à la lyonnaise*

Pommes *Macaire*
Consommé *au macaroni*
Ris de veau *à la macédoine*
Barbue *à la mâconnaise*
Pêches *Madame-Récamier*
Potage *Madeleine*
Jambon *au madère*
Langues de morue *à la madrilène*
Poularde *Maeterlinck*
Consommé *Magenta*

Filets de sole *Magny*
Salade *maharadjah*
Chicorée étuvée *au maigre*
Jambon *Maillot*
Fonds d'artichauts *Maintenon*
Pommes *Maire*
Pommes *à la maître d'hôtel*
Pouding *maïzena*
Potage *Malakoff*
Côtelettes d'agneau *Malmaison*
Croûte aux bananes *à la maltaise*
Poulet *Mancini*
Crème *Manon*
Carré d'agneau *à la maraîchère*
Entrecôte grillée *à la marchand de vins*
Côte de veau *à la maréchale*
Veau *Marengo*
Turbotin *Margot*
Pêches *Marguerite*
Filets de sole *Marguery*
Oeufs *Marianne*
Carottes *Maria-Stella*
Poulet *Marie-Antoinette*
Crème *Marie-Louise*
Crevettes *Marie-Rose*
Crème *Marie-Stuart*
Potage *Marigny*
Ragoût *à la marinière*
Filets de sole *Marivaux*
Noisettes de mouton *à la marocaine*
Punch *marquise*
Bouillabaisse *à la marseillaise*
Filets mignons *à la mascotte*
Tournedos *Masséna*

Oeufs brouillés *Massenet*
Anguille d'eau douce *à la matelote*
Barbeau *en matelote*
Filet de boeuf *Matignon*
Omelette *Maximilien*
Coquillettes *à la mayonnaise*
Coquilles Saint-Jacques *en mayonnaise*
Bombe *Médicis*
Coupe d'abricots *Melba*
Coquilles *à la ménagère*
Courgettes *à la mentonnaise*
Consommé *Mercédès*
Consommé *Messine*
Tartelettes *Metternich*
Darne de saumon *à la meunière*
Matelotte d'anguille *meurette*
Côtelettes d'agneau *à la mexicaine*
Oeufs *Meyerbeer*
Salade *mikado*
Choux de Bruxelles *à la milanaise*
Oeufs *mimosa*
Salmis de canard sauvage *à la minute*
Entrecôte *Mirabeau*
Homard *Miramar*
Poulet sauté *Mireille*
Soufflé de volaille *à la mirepoix*
Oeufs *Mirette*
Oeufs *miroir*
Boeuf *miroton*
Omelette *Mistral*
Côte de boeuf froide *à la mode*
Ballotine d'agneau *à la moderne*
Rouget *à la moelle*
Filets de sole *Moïna*

Perdreau *à la moldave*
Carré d'agneau *Monselet*
Tournedos *Montaigne*
Coupe *Mont-Blanc*
Cailles en caisses *Mont-Bry*
Pommes *Mont-Dore*
Consommé *Monte-Carlo*
Consommé *Montesquieu*
Bouchées *Montglas*
Sole *Montgolfier*
Bordure de riz *Montmorency*
Noisettes d'agneau *Montpensier*
Filets de sole *Montreuil*
Escalopes de foie gras *Montrouge*
Côte de veau *Morland*
Coquilles de cabillaud *Mornay*
Asperges blanches *à la sauce Mornay*
Bettes *à la mornay*
Petits pâtés *à la moscovite*
Poires glacées *Mourier*
Quenelles de brochet *mousselines*
Filets de sole *Murat*
Epaule de mouton *en musette*

Homard *à la nage*
Tomates farcies *Nana*
Beignets *Nanette*
Rouget *à la nantaise*
Barquettes d'huîtres *Nantua*
Timbales *à la nantuatienne*
Côte de veau *à la napolitaine*
Pommes *nature*
Poitrine de mouton grillée *au naturel*
Pommes *négresses*

Oeufs *à la neige*
Consommé *Nemours*
Consommé *Nemrod*
Biscuit glacé *Nesselrode*
Poularde *Néva*
Homard *Newburg*
Noisettes d'agneau *Nichette*
Médaillons d'anchois *à la niçoise*
Cailles *au nid*
Canapés *Ninon*
Oeufs mignons *à la nivernaise*
Filets mignons *Noailles*
Bûche *de Noël*
Velouté de crevettes *à la normande*
Bananes *à la norvégienne*
Ballotine de poularde *aux nouilles*
Tournedos *Novello*

Morue *à l'occitane*
Fruits rafraîchis *à l'occitanienne*
Bouillabaisse *de l'Océan*
Bombe *Odette*
Canapés *aux oeufs durs*
Oeufs brouillés *Offenbach*
Huîtres *en omelette*
Charlotte *Opéra*
Aubergines *à l'oranaise*
Mousse glacée *à l'orange*
Carré de mouton *à l'orientale*
Consommé *Orléans*
Noisettes *Orlov*
Filets de truite *Orly*
Fricandeau d'esturgeon *à l'oseille*
Oeufs *Oudinot*

Paupiettes de sole *Paillard*
Consommé *au pain*
Chicorée *en pain*
Soufflé *Palmyre*
Filets de sole *à la panetière*
Pâté chaud de saumon *en pantin*
Rouget *en papillote*
Haddock *au paprika*
Fromage bavarois *au parfait amour*
Allumettes *à la parisienne*
Côte de veau *Parmentier*
Filets de sole *Parmentière*
Consommé *à la parmesane*
Soufflé *au parmesan*
Pommes *Pascal*
Vacherin avec couronne
   en pâte d'amandes
Suprêmes de poulet *Patti*
Côtelettes d'agneau *Paul-Mounet*
Merlan *en paupiettes*
Céleri-rave farci *à la paysanne*
Turbot *à la pèlerine*
Noisettes *Pellissier*
Pêches *Pénélope*
Consommé *Pépita*
Poulet sauté *Périgord*
Chaussons *à la périgourdine*
Croquettes de foie gras
   à la sauce Périgueux
Côtelettes d'agneau *Périnette*
Salade *Pernollet*
Carpe à la juive *au persil*
Mou de veau *à la persillade*
Poulet sauté *Petit-Duc*

Asperges *en petits pois*
Risotto *à la piémontaise*
Potage *Pierre-le-Grand*
Aiguillettes de sole *Pierrot*
Filets de sole *en pilaf*
Côte de porc *Pilleverjus*
Tourte d'anchois *au pissalat*
Glace *à la pistache*
Epaule de mouton *en pistache*
Gâteau *de Pithiviers*
Sardines *au plat*
Glace *Plombières aux marrons*
Bifteck *à la poêle*
Betteraves *à la poitevine*
Côtelettes de chevreuil *poivrade*
Côtelettes de saumon *Pojarski*
Oeufs *Polignac*
Hachis de boeuf *à la polonaise*
Darne de saumon *au pommard*
Côtelettes de mouton *Pompadour*
Pommes frites *Pont-Neuf*
Côtelettes de mouton *en portefeuille*
Baron d'agneau *Porte-Maillot*
Caneton rouennais *au porto*
Harengs *à la portugaise*
Poularde *au pot*
Salade *Port-Royal*
Jambonneau *en potée*
Pieds de mouton *à la poulette*
Semoule *en pouding*
Tête de veau *en poupeton*
Crème glacée *au praliné*
Chou de printemps *à la presse*
Filet de boeuf *Prince-Albert*

Faisan *Prince-Orlov* à la gelée
Petits soufflés *à la princesse*
Consommé *Princesse-Alice*
Tartelettes *Printania*
Navarin de mouton *printanier*
Sauté d'agneau *à la printanière*
Tomates sautées *à la provençale*
Céleri-rave *en purée*

Tournedos *Quirinal*

Tourte froide d'anguille *Rabelais*
Poires *en rabotte*
Oeufs *Rachel*
Consommé *Rambouillet*
Salade *Raphaël*
Filets de maquereau *à la ravigote*
Côtelettes d'agneau *Réforme*
Cassolettes *Régence*
Tartelettes *Régina*
Dartois *à la reine*
Consommé *Reine-Jeanne*
Oeufs *Reine-Margot*
Jambon glacé *Reine-Pédauque*
Gâteau *Reine-de-Saba*
Consommé *Réjane*
Baron de mouton *Renaissance*
Baba *au rhum*
Bécasse *à la Riche*
Baron d'agneau *Richelieu*
Canapé *Riga*
Turbot *Riviera*
Turbot *Rivière*
Noisettes d'agneau *Rivoli*

Pêches meringuées *au riz*
Paupiettes de boeuf *au riz pilaf*
Pommes *en robe de chambre*
Pommes *en robe des champs*
Côte de porc *à la sauce Robert*
Filets de sole *La-Rochelle*
Crème *Rohan*
Beignets végétariens *à la romaine*
Fraises *Romanov*
Crêpes *au roquefort*
Poulet *Rose-Marie*
Poularde *Rosière*
Coquilles de volaille *Rossini*
Oeufs *Rothomago*
Soufflé *Rothschild*
Côtelettes d'agneau *à la rouennaise*
Homard *Rougemont*
Lièvre farci *à la royale*
Consommé *Rubens*
Harengs fumés *à la russe*

Oeufs brouillés *Sagan*
Petits pois *Saint-Cloud*
Omelette *Saint-Flour*
Escalopes de ris de veau
    Saint-Germain
Crème *Saint-Honoré*
Cromesquis *Saint-Hubert*
Turbot *à la Saint-Malo*
Cailles en cocotte *Saint-Mars*
Suprêmes de volaille *Saint-Saëns*
Faisan *Sainte-Alliance*
Ailerons de dindonneau *Sainte-Menehould*
Gras-double de boeuf *en salade*

Pigeonneau *en salmis*
Oeufs brouillés *au salpicon de homard*
Oeufs brouillés *au salpicon de langouste*
Oeufs *Sans-Gêne*
Potage *santé*
Sole *Sarah-Bernhardt*
Epaule de mouton *à la sarde*
Pommes *à la sarladaise*
Selle d'agneau *à la sarrasine*
Poularde au riz, *sauce suprême*
Pieds de mouton à la sauce *poulette*
Côtelettes de veau *en sauce tomate*
Poulet *Savary*
Fèves fraîches *à la sarriette*
Gâteau *de Savoie*
Gratin de pommes
    à la savoyarde
Pouding *saxon*
Escalope de veau *Serge*
Truffes *à la serviette*
Bouchées *Sévigné*
Ravioli *à la sibérienne*
Macaroni *à la sicilienne*
Coupe *Singapour*
Carré de porc *à la soissonnaise*
Potage *Solférino*
Poulet farci *à la mode de Sorges*
Fonds d'artichauts farcis *Soubise*
Marrons *en soufflé*
Truffes *sous la cendre*
Cailles *sous les cendres*
Foie gras *Souvarov*
Poularde *Stanley*
Filet de boeuf froid *à la strasbourgeoise*

Carrelet *Suchet*
Epinards *au sucre*
Filets d'anchois *à la suédoise*
Omelette *à la suissesse*
Poularde *Sully*
Velouté de volaille *sultane*
Pommes *surprise*
Melon rafraîchi *en surprise*
Crêpes *Suzette*
Filets de sole *Sylvette*
Pêches *sur canapés*
Oeufs durs *sur chicorée*
Noisette de pré-salé *sur croûtons*
Rognons de boeuf *sur gazon*
Lactaires *sur le gril*
Oeufs durs *sur macédoine de légumes*
Barbue *sur le plat*
Oeufs durs *sur purée de champignons*

Fondants de foie gras *à la Taillevent*
Côtelettes d'agneau *Talleyrand*
Consommé *Talma*
Pouding *au tapioca*
Coquilles Saint-Jacques frites *à la tartare*
Cabillaud frit à l'anglaise, *sauce tartare*
Lièvre *en terrine*
Tête de veau *Tertillière*
Filets de sole *en torsade*
Ragoût *à la tortue*
Ailerons de dindonneau *en tortue*
Bombe *Tosca*
Poularde *à la toscane*
Filets de barbue *à la toulonnaise*

Aubergines au gratin *à la toulousaine*
Truite de rivière en matelote *à la tourangelle*
Colin frit *en tranches*
Bananes *Tredern*
Consommé *Trianon*
Homard *Trouville*
Filets de sole *à la trouvillaise*
Poularde *aux truffes*
Rognons de mouton *Turbigo*
Côtelettes d'agneau *à la turque*
Noisettes de mouton *à la tyrolienne*
Fruits rafraîchis *tzarine*

Côtelettes de chevreuil *d'Uzès*

Noisettes d'agneau *Valenciennes*
Homard *Valençay*
Croquettes de macaroni *à la valentinoise*
Bombe *Valérien*
Potage *Valéry*
Entrecôte grillée *à la sauce Valois*
Rissoles de truffes *Valromey*
Pommes *à la vapeur*
Paupiettes d'agneau *Vatel*
Poulet *Vauban*
Truite de rivière *à la vauclusienne*
Gourilos *au velouté*
Chouée *vendéenne*
Barbue *à la vénitienne*
Oeufs *Verdier*
Cerneaux *au verjus*
Consommé *au vermicelle*
Filets de barbue *Véron*

Bombe *Véronique*
Paupiettes de saumon *au vert*
Choux *au vert-pré*
Carottes *Vichy*
Consommé *Victor-Emmanuel II*
Purée *Victor-Hugo*
Coquilles de saumon *Victoria*
Carré d'agneau frit *à la viennoise*
Perdreau *à la vigneronne*
Côtelettes de mouton *à la villageoise*
Filets de sole *Villaret*
Artichauts farcis *Villars*
Poulet sauté *Villeneuve*
Attereaux de homard *à la sauce Villeroi*
Escalopes de ris de veau *Villeroi*
Poireaux *à la vinaigrette*
Cerises *au vinaigre*
Anguille marinée *au vin blanc*

Oie *à la mode de Visé*
Pommes *Voisin*
Consommé *Voltaire*
Galantine d'anguille *en volute*
Côte de porc *à la vosgienne*

Filets de sole *Waleska*
Oeufs mollets *Washington*
Allumettes *Wladimir*

Potage *Xavier*
Gratin de scampi *au xérès*

Pommes *à la yorkaise*
Pommes *Yvette*

Croûtes *à la zingara*

PART FOUR

VOCABULARY

abricot (m)	apricot
agneau (m)	lamb
agneau de lait (m)	milk-fed lamb
aigrefin (m)	haddock (alternative spellings: aiglefin, égrefin, églefin)
aiguillette (f)	thin strip of meat
ail (m)	garlic
aileron (m)	winglet
allumette (f)	small rectangle of puff paste, garnished in different ways and cooked in the oven
alose (f)	shad
alouette (f)	skylark
aloyau (m)	sirloin of beef
amande (f)	almond
amourettes (f. pl)	spinal marrow
ananas (m)	pineapple
anchois (m)	anchovy
andouille (f)	chitterling sausage
andouillette (f)	small chitterling sausage
anguille (f)	eel
aromate (m)	aromatic, spice
animelles (f.pl)	lamb's fry
artichaut (m)	artichoke (globe)
asperge (f)	asparagus
aspic (m)	aspic
assiette (f)	plate
attereau (m)	skewer, the food cooked on a skewer
aubergine (f)	aubergine, egg-plant
aveline (f)	hazel-nut
avoine (f)	oats
baba (m)	small cake made of raised paste, often containing raisins, and steeped in rum or kirsch syrup
bacon (m)	smoked bacon

ballotine (f)	butcher's meat, boned and rolled without any kind of stuffing; by extension, it is used to denote a *galantine*; also, a roll of stuffed cabbage
banane (f)	banana
bar (m)	sea-perch
barbeau (m)	barbel
barbillon (m)	barbel
barbue (f)	brill
barigoule (f)	kind of mushroom
baron (m)	saddle and two legs of lamb or beef
barquette (f)	boat-shaped pastry-case or canapé
basilic (m)	basil
bavarois (m)	kind of blanc-mange using *crème à l'anglaise* and whipped cream
bavette (f)	skirt of beef
béatilles (f.pl)	old name for cock's comb, kidney, sweetbread and mushrooms, bound with *velouté* sauce or *sauce suprême* and used as garnish
bécasse (f)	woodcock
bécassine (f)	snipe
beignet (m)	fritter
bette (f)	beet, chard
betterave (f)	beetroot
beurre (m)	butter
biarrotte (f)	garnish comprising flap mushrooms and small potato cakes
bifteck (m)	beef steak
bigarade (f)	bitter orange
bigarreau (m)	white-heart cherry
biscuit (m)	biscuit
bisque (f)	thick shell-fish stew
blanc	white
blanchaille (f)	whitebait
blanquette (f)	white meat stew

blé (m)	corn
boeuf (m)	beef
bombe (f)	ice pudding
bordure (f)	border
bouchée (f)	small patty
boudin blanc (m)	white sausage
boudin noir (m)	black pudding
bouillabaisse (f)	Mediterranean fish stew
boulette (f)	shaped like a small ball
bouton bruxellois (m)	Brussels sprout (small)
brandade (f)	preparation of salt-cod pounded with oil, garlic and cream
brème (f)	bream
brioche (f)	brioche, type of cottage loaf made with fine flour, butter and eggs
broche (f)	spit
brochette (f)	skewer, food cooked on skewer
brocoli (m)	broccoli
brouillé	scrambled
brugnon (m)	nectarine
bûche (f)	log
cabillaud (m)	cod (fresh)
cacao (m)	cocoa
cadgéry (m)	kedgeree
café (m)	coffee
caille (f)	quail
caisse (f)	oval paper case; sometimes, small, round or oval
or caissette (f)	receptacle used for cooking or serving
canapé (m)	canapé
canard (m)	duck
canard sauvage (m)	wild duck
caneton (m)	duckling
cannelon (m)	rectangular hors-d'oeuvre in puff paste

cannelloni (m)	a stuffed pasta preparation
capilotade (f)	ragoût, stew
câpre (f)	caper
caramel (m)	caramel
carbonnade (f)	meat stewed in beer
cardon (m)	cardoon
caroline (f)	small savoury éclair
carotte (f)	carrot
carpe (f)	carp
carré d'agneau (m)	best-end of lamb
carrelet (m)	dab, plaice
cartouche (f)	round piece of grease-proof paper; in *poires cartouches*, same as *rabotte*
cassolette (f)	small case filled with dressing
cassoulet (m)	stew of beans and meat
caviar (m)	caviar
céleri (m)	celery
céleri-rave (m)	celeriac
cendre (f)	cinder, wood-ash
cèpe (m)	flap mushroom
cerfeuil (m)	chervil
cerise (f)	cherry
cerneau (m)	green walnut
cervelas (m)	saveloy
cervelle (f)	brains
champ (m)	field
champignon (m)	mushroom
chanterelle (f)	cantharellus mushroom
chapon (m)	capon
charlotte (f)	charlotte
chateaubriand (m)	double fillet steak
chaud	warm, hot
chaud-froid (m)	(poultry) covered with a *chaud-froid* sauce
chausson (m)	turnover

chevreuil (m)	roebuck
chicorée (f)	endive
chiffonnade (f)	long thin shreds, often of lettuce
chocolat (m)	chocolate
ciboulette (f)	chive
chou (m)	cabbage
chou de Bruxelles (m)	Brussels sprout
choucroute (f)	sauerkraut
chou-fleur (m)	cauliflower
chou-rave (m)	kohl-rabi
chou-rouge (m)	red cabbage
citron (m)	lemon
civet (m)	stew, often translated by 'jugged'
clavaire (f)	club-top mushroom
cocktail (m)	cocktail
cocotte (f)	fire-proof earthenware dish
coeur (m)	heart
colin (m)	hake
collerette (f)	ring; sometimes ring-shaped with scalloped edge
colombine (f)	tart-shaped hors-d'oeuvre in semolina paste and parmesan cheese case
comice (f)	Comice pear
compote (f)	stewed fruit, compote of stewed fruit
concombre (m)	cucumber
confit	preserved
confit (m)	conserve
confiture (f)	jam
consommé (m)	clarified soup
contre-filet (m)	boned sirloin of beef
copeau (m)	shaving
coq (m)	cockerel
coque (à la)	boiled (egg)
coquillage (m)	shell-fish, preparation served in a shell

coquille (f)	shell
coquille Saint-Jacques (f)	scollop
coquillette (f)	shell-shaped paste case
cornet (m)	cornet, cornet-shaped
cornichon (m)	gherkin
côte (f)	rib, chop
côtelette (f)	cutlet
coulemelle (f)	kind of mushroom
coupe (f)	cup of fruit, cream and ice-cream
courge (f)	gourd
courgette (f)	vegetable marrow
couronne (f)	crown, crown-shaped
court-bouillon (m)	stock for cooking fish
crabe (m)	crab
crème (f)	cream, cream soup
crêpe (f)	pancake
crépine (f)	caul
crépinette (f)	meat cake wrapped in caul
cresson (m)	cress
crête (f)	cockscomb, crest-shaped
crevette grise (f)	shrimp
crevette rose (f)	prawn
cromesquis (m)	kromesky
croquette (f)	croquette
croustade (f)	pastry case
croûte (f)	slice of toast or fried bread; flan case
croûton (m)	slice of toast or fried bread; sippet
cuiller (cuillère) (f)	spoon
cuisse (f)	leg, thigh of chicken
cuissot (m)	leg, haunch
culotte (f)	rump of beef
currie, cari (m)	curry
darne (f)	thick slice of fish

dartois (m)	small rectangle of puff paste garnished in a variety of ways
daube (f)	stew of meat in red wine
daurade, dorade (f)	dorado
délicieuse (f)	small fried cheese ball
demi-pamplemousse (m)	half a grapefruit
dessert (m)	dessert
desserte (f)	left-overs
diablotin (m)	small round of bread, garnished with cheese and gratinated
dinde (f)	turkey hen
dindonneau (m)	young turkey
double d'agneau (m)	the two hindquarters of lamb
douillon (m)	preparation consisting of a fruit (a pear, for example), covered with lining paste and cooked
doux, douce	sweet, mild

eau (f)	water
eau douce (f)	fresh water
eau de mer (f)	sea water
eau-de-vie (f)	brandy
écarlate	scarlet
échalote (f)	shallot
échine (f)	chine
éclair (m)	long bun made of choux paste
églefin (m)	see *aigrefin*
émincés (m.pl)	dish prepared from thin slices of meat or fruit
endive (f)	chicory
entrecôte (f)	beef steak cut from the ribs
épaule (f)	shoulder
éperlan (m)	smelt
épigramme (f)	compressed breast of lamb, cut into diamond shape, covered with egg and breadcrumbs, and tossed in butter
épinard (m)	spinach
escabèche (f)	hors-d'oeuvre of cold fish (fried), marinaded in a court-bouillon
escalope (f)	scollop (of veal)
escargot (m)	snail
estouffade (f)	brown meat stock
estouffat (m)	Languedoc word for *étuvé*
estragon (m)	tarragon
esturgeon (m)	sturgeon
étuvé (m)	stew
faisan (m)	pheasant
farce (f)	stuffing, forcemeat
farine (f)	flour
fenouil (m)	fennel
feuilleton (m)	fillet of veal, stuffed and cooked (cut into thin slices and wrapped in caul)

fève (f)	bean
figue (f)	fig
filet (m)	fillet
filet mignon (m)	tenderloin
fin, fine	fine, thin, choice
fines herbes (f.pl)	mixed herbs
flan (m)	flan
flétan (m)	halibut
fleur (f)	flower
flottant	floating
foie (m)	liver
foie gras (m)	fatted liver (goose, duck etc.)
fondant (m)	fondant
fonds d'artichaut (m)	artichoke bottom
fondu	melted
fondue (f)	preparation based on melting down of a vegetable or cheese etc.
fouetté	whipped
four (m)	oven

frais, fraîche	fresh
fraise (f)	strawberry
fraise de veau (f)	calf's crow
framboise (f)	raspberry
frangipane (f)	frangipane (kind of almond cream or paste)
frappé	chilled
fressure (f)	pluck of an animal
fricadelle (f)	fried meat ball
fricandeau (m)	braised joint of silverside
fricassée (f)	white ragoût
fritot (m)	small deep-fried fritter
froid	cold
fromage (m)	cheese
fruit (m)	fruit
fruits confits (m)	preserved fruits
fruits de mer (m)	ensemble of shell-fish
fumet (m)	essence, often of carcase gravy plus *fine champagne*
galantine (f)	boned poultry, stuffed, cooked and served cold
galette (f)	small, round, flat cake
garenne (f)	warren
gâteau (m)	cake, pudding
gaufre (f)	waffle
gaufrette (f)	wafer biscuit
gazon (m)	turf
gelée (f)	jelly
genièvre (m)	juniper
gibelotte (f)	hare or rabbit fricassée with red or white wine
gibier (m)	game
gigot (m)	leg of lamb
girolle (f)	cantharellus mushroom
glace (f)	ice, ice-cream
glacé	iced, glazed

gnocchi (m)	gnocchi
gombos (m)	gombo, okra
gorenflot (m)	hexagonal entremets in baba paste
goujon (m)	gudgeon
goujonnade (f)	dish in which fish is prepared to resemble gudgeon in size
goulash, gulyas (m)	goulash
gourilos (m)	stump of endive
gras-double (m)	tripe
gratin (m)	dish that is gratinated
grenadin (m)	small, larded slice of veal fillet
grenouille (f)	frog
gril (m)	grill
grive (f)	thrush
grondin (m)	gurnard, gurnet
groseille (f)	currant, berry (red, black, goose)
hachis (m)	mince
haddock (m)	smoked haddock
halicot de mouton (m)	mutton stew
hareng (m)	herring
hareng saur (m)	red herring
haricot (m)	bean
herbe (f)	grass, herb
hérisson (m)	hedgehog (*pommes en hérisson*, apples with almonds stuck in to resemble hedgehog)
hirondelle (f)	swallow
hochepot (m)	stew of meat and vegetables
homard (m)	lobster
hors-d'oeuvre (m)	hors-d'oeuvre
huile (f)	oil
huître (f)	oyster
île (f)	isle, island

jambon (m)	ham
jambonneau (m)	hamkin
jarret (m)	knuckle
joue (f)	cheek
jus (m)	juice, gravy
kari, currie, cari (m)	curry
kougelhof (m)	an Alsatian pastry
krapfen (m)	round, fried pastry sandwich filled with jam
lactaire (f)	type of mushroom
lait (m)	milk
laitance (f)	soft roe
laitue (f)	lettuce
lambic (m)	Lambick, Belgian beer
lamproie (f)	lamprey
langouste (f)	spiny lobster, crawfish
langoustine (f)	Dublin Bay prawn, Norway lobster
langue (f)	tongue
lapereau (m)	young rabbit
lapin (m)	rabbit
lard (m)	bacon
légume (m)	vegetable
lentille (f)	lentil
lépiote (f)	variety of mushroom
lièvre (m)	hare
limande (f)	dab
longe (f)	loin
lorgnette (f)	opera glasses (i.e., the shape of these)
lotte de mer (f)	burbot
macaroni (m)	macaroni
macédoine (f)	diced mixture of fruit or vegetables
au maigre	prepared without butcher's meat

maïs (m)	maize, sweet corn
mandarine (f)	tangerine
mange-tout (m)	sugar pea
maquereau (m)	mackerel
marbre (m)	marble
marchand (m)	merchant
Mardi gras (m)	Shrove Tuesday
marquise (f)	iced drink, marquise pear
marron (m)	sweet chestnut
matelote (f)	fish stew with red or white wine
mauviette (f)	lark
médaillon (m)	medallion-shaped piece of meat
melon (m)	melon
menthe (f)	mint
mer (f)	sea
meringue (f)	meringue
merlan (m)	whiting
mirabelle (f)	mirabelle plum
miroton (m)	stew of left-overs of meat
moelle (f)	bone-marrow
moka (m)	Mocha coffee
mollet	fairly soft
morille (f)	morel (kind of mushroom)
morue (f)	salt cod
mou de veau (m)	lungs of calf
moule (f)	mussel
moulé	moulded
mousse (f)	preparation whipped into a foamy consistency
mousseline (f)	mousse containing whipped cream
mousseron (m)	small mushroom
moutarde (f)	mustard
mouton (m)	sheep, mutton
mulet (m)	mullet
mûre (f)	mulberry

mûre sauvage (f)	blackberry, bramble
myrtille (f)	bilberry
navarin (m)	mutton or lamb stew
navet (m)	turnip

neige (f)	snow
nid (m)	nest
noir	black
noisette (f)	hazel-nut, small, round cut of meat (lamb or mutton)
noisette	nut-brown colour, hazel-nut shape
noix (f)	walnut
nonat (m)	small Mediterranean fish
nonne (f)	nun
nouille (f)	noodle
nouillette (f)	small noodle
nouveau, nouvelle	new

oeuf (m)	egg
oeuf brouillé (m)	scrambled egg
oeuf en cocotte (m)	egg baked in a fire-proof dish
oeuf à la coque (m)	boiled egg
oeuf dur (m)	hard-boiled egg
oeuf mignon (m)	egg-shaped preparation of duchess potatoes
oeuf mollet (m)	fairly soft boiled egg
oeuf moulé (m)	moulded egg
oie (f)	goose
oignon (m)	onion
olive (f)	olive
omelette (f)	omelette
orange (f)	orange
oreille (f)	ear
orge (f)	barley
ortolan (m)	ortolan bunting
oseille (f)	sorrel
paille (f)	straw
paillette (f)	thin straw
pain (m)	bread, loaf (i.e., the shape of a loaf)
pamplemousse (m)	grapefruit
panais (m)	parsnip
pantin (m)	oval or rectangular pie
pannequet (m)	small pancake
papillote (f)	heart-shaped oiled paper case
paprika (m)	paprika
parfait (m)	perfumed ice pudding, foie gras served in jelly
pascal	Paschal
patate (f)	sweet potato
pâte (f)	paste
pâté (m)	pie, patty (also the shape of a pie)
pâtes (f.pl)	pasta
paupiette (f)	preparation rolled to shape of large cork

pavé (m)	square or rectangular shaped preparation (mousse, pastry etc.)
pêche (f)	peach
perdreau (m)	young partridge
perdrix (f)	partridge
perle (f)	pearl
perlée (orge)	pearl (barley)
persil (m)	parsley
petit	small
petit pain (m)	bread roll
petits pois (m.pl)	garden peas
petit-salé (m)	pickled pork
pièce de boeuf (f)	point of rump of beef
pied (m)	foot, trotter
pied-de-mouton (m)	kind of mushroom

pigeon (m)	pigeon
pigeonneau (m)	young pigeon
piment doux (m)	sweet pimento
pintade (f)	guinea-fowl
pistache (f)	pistachio
plat	flat
plat (m)	dish
plie (f)	plaice
plomb (m)	lead
pluvier (m)	plover
poché	poached
pointe d'asperge (f)	asparagus tip
poire (f)	pear
poireau (m)	leek
pois cassés (m.pl)	split peas
pois chiches (m)	chick peas
poisson (m)	fish
poitrine (f)	breast
poivre (m)	pepper
pommard (m)	Pommard wine
pomme (f)	apple; often short for *pomme de terre*
pomme de terre (f)	potato
pomponnette (f)	small, purse-shaped rissole served as hors-d'oeuvre
porc (m)	pork, pig
portefeuille (f)	wallet
pot (m)	pot
potage (m)	soup
pot-au-feu (m)	bouillon with garnish of meat and vegetables
potée (f)	kind of soup made with pork and vegetables
potiron (m)	pumpkin
pouding (m)	pudding
poularde (f)	fattened young hen
poulet (m)	chicken

poulet de grain (m)	corn-fed chicken
poupeton (m)	preparation consisting of rolled meat
pourpier (m)	purslane
poussin (m)	spring chicken
praliné	decorated or flavoured with *pralin*
pralin (m)	pounded almond toffee
pré-salé (m)	salt-meadow lamb
primeurs (m.pl)	early or forced vegetables
printemps (m)	Spring
profiterole (f)	small, spherical preparation of choux paste
prune (f)	plum
pruneau (m)	prune
puits (m)	well
pur	pure
purée (f)	purée, thick, sieved soup
quartier (m)	quarter
quenelle (f)	ball-shaped preparation
queue (f)	tail
râble (m)	saddle of hare
rabotte (f)	fruit covered with lining paste
racine (f)	root (vegetable)
radis (m)	radish
rafraîchi	chilled, cooled, refreshed
ragoût (m)	stew of game or butcher's meat
raie (f)	skate
raifort (m)	horse-radish
raisin (m)	grape
ramequin (m)	tartlet filled with cream cheese
ravioli (m)	ravioli
reine (f)	queen
reinette (f)	pippin
rémoulade (f)	sharp, garnished mayonnaise sauce

rhubarbe (f)	rhubarb
rhum (m)	rum
rillauds (m.pl) ⎫ rillettes (f.pl) ⎬ rillons (m.pl) ⎭	pork, fatty and lean, cut into small pieces, cooked and crushed when cold, used as hors-d'oeuvre
ris d'agneau (m)	lamb's sweetbreads
ris de veau (m)	calf's sweetbreads
risotto (m)	risotto
rissole (f)	rissole
riz (m)	rice
rivière (f)	river
robe (f)	dress, skin of potato etc.
robe de chambre (f)	dressing-gown; skin of potato etc.
rocher (m)	rock
rognon (m)	kidney
rollmop (m)	hors-d'oeuvre consisting of fillets of herring rolled round cucumber or chopped onion, pierced with cocktail stick and pickled
romsteck (m)	rump steak
rosbif (m)	roast beef
rôti (m)	roast
rouelle (f)	round slice
rouge	red
rouget (m)	red mullet
roulade (f)	rolled slice of stuffed meat etc.
sabayon (m)	beaten egg, sugar and wine, liqueur or spirit
sagou (m)	sago
saint-pierre (m)	John Dory
saison (f)	season
salade (f)	salad (often used to mean simply lettuce)
salami (m)	salami
salé	salted, salt
salep (m)	salep (meal from dried tubers of orchid plants)

salmis (m)	stew of feathered game
salpicon (m)	preparation consisting of one or more elements cut into small dice and bound with a sauce
salsifis (m)	salsify, oyster-plant
sang (m)	blood
sanglier (m)	wild boar
sardine (f)	sardine
sauce (f)	sauce
saucisse (f)	sausage
saucisson (m)	preserved sausage
saumon (m)	salmon
saumoné	salmon-coloured
sauté (m)	preparation made by tossing ingredients in butter etc.
sauvage	wild, uncultivated
savarin (m)	cake in raised paste, soaked in flavoured syrup, then sprinkled with kirsch or rum
scampi (m)	scampi
sec, sèche	dry, dried
sel (m)	salt
selle (f)	saddle
semoule (f)	semolina

serviette (f)	serviette, napkin
sirop (m)	syrup
sole (f)	sole
sorbet (m)	flavoured water ice
soufflé (m)	soufflé
soupe (f)	soup
soupir (m)	chou paste fritter (lit. a sigh)
spaghetti (m)	spaghetti
subric (m)	croquette-like hors-d'oeuvre
sucre (m)	sugar
suprême (m)	name used to designate a dish arranged in fine style; the fillet of a fish or from the breast of poultry
talmouse (f)	kind of cheese tartlet served as hors-d'oeuvre
tapioca (m)	tapioca
tarte (f)	tart
tartelette (f)	tartlet
tasse (f)	cup
tendron (m)	breast of veal
terrine (f)	earthenware dish for cooking or service; also denotes food cooked in such a dish and served cold
tête (f)	head
thé (m)	tea
thon (m)	tunny
timbale (f)	drum-shaped preparation in pastry with various fillings; hemispherical container
tomate (f)	tomato
topinambour (m)	Jerusalem artichoke
torrent (m)	torrent, mountain stream
torsade (f)	cable, twist
tortue (f)	turtle herb
tournedos (m)	round of steak cut off long fillet
tourte (f)	tart

tourteau (m)	edible crab
tranche (f)	slice
tripes (f.pl)	tripe
tronçon (m)	thick slice of fish
truffe (f)	truffle
truffé	garnished or stuffed with truffles
truite (f)	trout
turbot (m)	turbot
turbotin (m)	young turbot
vacherin (m)	entremets formed of rings of meringue on thin, sweet pastry, garnished with Chantilly or double cream (sometimes almond paste is used instead of meringue)
vanille (f)	vanilla
vanneau (m)	lapwing
vapeur (f)	steam
veau (m)	veal, calf
velours (m)	velvet
velouté (m)	soup thickened with egg-yolk or double cream
vermicelle (m)	vermicelli
verjus (m)	verjuice (acid liquor from sour fruit)
vert	green
viande (f)	meat
vin (m)	wine
vinaigre (m)	vinegar
vivant	living, alive
volaille (f)	poultry; used for chicken not served whole
vol-au-vent (m)	oval or round puff pastry case with various fillings
xérès (m)	sherry
yaourt (m)	yoghourt